T0269977

**Also by John Tamny**

*When Politicians Panicked: The New Coronavirus,
Expert Opinion, and a Tragic Lapse of Reason*

# BRINGING ADAM SMITH
*into the*
# AMERICAN HOME

*A Case Against Home Ownership*

JACK RYAN & JOHN TAMNY

Post Hill
PRESS

A POST HILL PRESS BOOK
ISBN: 979-8-88845-194-6
ISBN (eBook): 979-8-88845-195-3

Bringing Adam Smith into the American Home:
A Case Against Home Ownership
© 2024 by John Tamny & Jack Ryan
All Rights Reserved

Cover design by Conroy Accord

Post Hill Press
New York • Nashville
posthillpress.com

Published in the United States of America
1 2 3 4 5 6 7 8 9 10

# DEDICATIONS

To my mom and dad, Amanda my wife, and John
Tamny—an intellect of the highest order

—Jack Ryan


For my wife Kendall, who taught me so much about
housing, home ownership, and its myriad flaws
through her tireless search for the house we live in.

—John Tamny

# CONTENTS

Introduction...........................................................................ix

Chapter 1:  Despite What They Tell You, Housing
            Is Not Investment...............................................1

Chapter 2:  Housing Consumption and the Low
            Interest Rate Myth...........................................13

Chapter 3:  That Which Holds People in Place
            Restrains Economic Progress ...........................29

Chapter 4:  The NAR Cartel's Obnoxious Tax on Progress....39

Chapter 5:  What Boosts Human Capital Mobility
            Will Also Lift Realtors and the
            Economy at Large.............................................53

Chapter 6:  High Housing Sales Commissions
            Restrict Investment, and by Extension,
            Job Creation.....................................................69

Chapter 7:  My Talent, and My Choice of What to
            Do with It ........................................................81

Chapter 8:   A Case Against Home Ownership ....................91

Conclusion.........................................................................103

Afterword:   Adam Smith Can Only Work in Free Markets....113

Endnotes..........................................................................146

Acknowledgments by John Tamny .....................................151

# INTRODUCTION

*"Though a house, therefore, may yield a revenue to its proprietor, and thereby serve in the function of a capital to him, it cannot yield any to the public, nor serve in the function of a capital to it, and the revenue of the whole body of the people can never be in the smallest degree increased by it."*

– Adam Smith, *The Wealth of Nations*, p. 305

"House Price Horror Show." The latter blared from the cover of *The Economist* magazine's October 22, 2022, issue. Sadly for homeowners and the housing sector more broadly, *The Economist's* pessimistic take was in some ways a late entry to an ongoing wake. In other words, a "horror show" having to do with housing was no longer fresh news.

Just a month before a front-page article in the *Wall Street Journal* came with the title "Housing Market Stumps

Forecasters." Inside the article the news was worse than the headline. "Home sales have plunged."[1]

Only for the housing market to continue its decline. By year-end of 2022, home sales had declined for a 10th straight month.[2] A 20 percent fall in housing transactions said to be born of rising interest rates was fingered as the problem,[3] but then conventional wisdom on the matter of housing or anything economic has been known to be wrong. The main thing is that compared to where housing had been, its 2022 correction was more than a bit startling.

Former Citigroup CEO Chuck Prince famously observed ahead of 2008's convulsions that "as long as the music is playing, you've got to get up and dance." Prince was vilified for realistically stating the obvious about businesses being in the business of profit, but whatever the true context of Prince's quip to the *Wall Street Journal,* a basic truism of real estate is that "the music always stops." And so it seemingly stopped once again in 2022. How quickly things had changed.

The outlook for owning a home had just a year before been defined by "fever" or "mania." We won't say "bubble" because the latter is a lazy word that presumes markets comprised solely of buyers. Still, amid a dampening in the housing market that some referred to as a "plunge" was quite the contrast to where the market had been not too long ago. Which is where we'll pivot to as we begin this book.

\* \* \*

"Remember back in March when you couldn't find toilet paper? That's what buying a home feels like these days." Those were the words of a Washington, DC-based real estate agent. It was September of 2020, and housing was all the rage not just in the nation's capital, but across the country.

Demand for housing had increased well beyond supply of same. By June of 2021, housing inventory had plummeted 21 percent compared to the previous year, and as a consequence the few houses for sale were being snapped up in in record time. While creatively financed mortgages in many ways defined the housing market of the early 2000s, "all-cash offers" were the story of 2020–21.[4]

Given the lack of inventory relative to feverish demand, sellers had choices. They would take the cash up front from eager buyers, thank you very much.

If you're reading this book, you likely have an interest in housing, housing markets or markets themselves, which means you remember the period well. Possibly even more broadly, you may have an interest in how markets in general can go badly wrong when subsidized, cartelized, and when surrounded by emotionalism. The emotional and almost patriotic call to own a home stems mostly from those who benefit from its subsidization and cartelization. This housing jingoism averts consumers' minds from the actual costs and benefits of the home. In fact, the housing market is a perfect petri dish to explore what can go wrong when a market is subsidized, cartelized and subject to heavy emotional overlays from politicians and trade groups.

While we'll make a case in future chapters that the sources of the 2020–21 housing mania were more varied than the pundit class realized, the consensus at the time was that a rapidly spreading virus (COVID-19) had changed everything. In particular, it had made working from home a possibility for a high percentage of Americans, and all too many jumped at the chance.

As a consequence, demand for housing well away from formerly bustling downtowns was the story. Increasingly fast internet speeds paired with of-the-moment companies like Zoom made working from anywhere far more realistic than it had been back in the days of slower, frequently dial-up internet. In the early 2000s some proclaimed "the death of distance" only for rumors of the demise of the office to prove greatly exaggerated. At least to the talking heads in the 2020s, "this time was different," which meant that apartment-dense cities were out while detached, suburban houses were in.

The view here is that, as is so often the case, a pundit class whose members suddenly found themselves working from home started "talking their own books" as it were. Remote work became doable for those reporting the news, only for demand for remote housing to soar. Instant correlation? We say curb your enthusiasm. While we don't deny the correlation, we think there was quite a bit more at work.

Indeed, 2020–21 was hardly the first time that demand for housing became manic stateside. The housing market has raged at varying levels of excitement throughout American history. As historian Niall Ferguson described it in his 2008 book, *The Ascent of Money*, property is "the English-speaking world's favorite economic game." In Ferguson's estimation, "No other facet of financial life has such a hold on the popular imagination."[5] Or, as Pa Bailey explained it to Jimmy Stewart's George Bailey in the 1946 film *It's a Wonderful Life*, home ownership is a "fundamental urge," it's "deep in the race for a man to want to own his own roof and walls and fireplace." Yes, when housing soared amid COVID confusion it was most certainly a movie Americans had seen before. When it comes to housing, the American appetite has long been gargantuan.

Yet despite a relentless American appetite for property, politicians have long made a point of subsidizing the "fundamental urge." And no, this hasn't been a Democrat or Republican thing; rather, the leading lights of both parties have long gone out of their way to make home ownership a very preferred activity in the eyes of Washington.

During the presidency of Franklin Delano Roosevelt, the Home Owners' Loan Corporation was created to stretch the terms of loans to as long as fifteen years in order to reduce the monthly burden of mortgages. Notable here is that under FDR's Republican predecessor, Herbert Hoover, the Federal Home Loan Bank Board had already been given life in order to encourage mortgage issuance by Savings and Loans (S&Ls). FDR also rolled out federal deposit insurance to make savers more comfortable about loaning S&Ls their unspent wealth that would be transferred to home buyers.[6]

In 1977, Democratic president Jimmy Carter signed into law the Community Reinvestment Act (CRA), which required the Federal Reserve and other banking regulators on the federal level "to encourage financial institutions to help meet the credit needs of the communities in which they do business, including low and moderate income neighborhoods."[7] Fast forward to 1995, in the words of the conservative editorialists at *Investor's Business Daily*, President Bill Clinton turned the CRA "into an aggressive program that basically forced banks to lend money to 'underserved' communities" where borrowers didn't necessarily have the means to pay back monies borrowed.[8]

The Taxpayer Relief Act of 1997 revealed further favoritism on the part of Clinton for housing. The act essentially zeroed out capital gains taxes on home sales since the first $500,000 in profits were exempt from the tax. In a preview of the tax act bruited at the 1996 Democratic National Convention, Clinton made clear his vision that "if you sell your home, you will not have to pay a capital gains tax on it ever — not ever."[9]

Eager to add financial muscle to what his administration was trying to achieve, Clinton empowered Housing and Urban Development (HUD) secretary Andrew Cuomo, HUD the regulator of Fannie Mae and Freddie Mac, to pressure the federal government-sponsored agencies about their lending. Their goal in 2000 would be to make over $1 trillion in new loans to low- and moderate-income borrowers.[10]

Those Democrats sure are generous with the money of others? Not so fast. As we made clear previously, the housing obsession of the American people is shared by the American political class, and without regard to political party.

While Republicans made hay of the Clinton administration's efforts to boost mortgage lending for "those with low incomes who couldn't necessarily repay a loan," it was Republican president Gerald Ford who signed the Home Mortgage Disclosure Act into law in 1975. In a very real sense a preview of the CRA, the act signed by Ford "aimed to fight discrimination in lending by requiring banks to disclose details of their customers."[11] As Alan Greenspan derisively put it about the wrongheaded legislation, the act implied that "an efficient capital market is undesirable and that allocation of credit by political group pressures is superior."[12] It seems the GOP is pretty free and easy with the money of others too…

And it didn't stop there. When George H. W. Bush was elected president in 1988, he appointed Jack Kemp as HUD secretary. Kemp demanded a pretty wide-ranging portfolio that included what he saw as a more market-friendly "War on Poverty." Of the main bullets he laid out for his war, two involved housing. HUD would work to "Expand Homeownership and Affordable Housing Opportunities," and also "Enforce Fair Housing for All."[13] Kemp threatened to resign when there was resistance inside the Bush administration to his call for $1 billion to fund a program he titled Home Ownership for People Everywhere.[14]

George W. Bush followed Bill Clinton into the White House and very quickly talked up his vision for an "ownership society." As readers can probably imagine, the vision included increased home ownership care of the taxpayer. In Bush's words, "We want everybody in America to own their own home."

In 2003, Bush giddily signed the American Dream Downpayment Act, which would subsidize first-time home-buyers primarily from low-income groups. The rhetorically free-market Bush administration backed up the legislation by leaning on lenders to make sure they weren't overly intrusive when it came to asking subprime borrowers for full documentation when it came to securing loans. After which the Bush HUD, much like the Clinton HUD, pressured Fannie Mae and Freddie Mac to support subprime lending.[15] Meet the new boss, same as the old boss…? Don't worry, it gets worse.

A year earlier, the Bush administration was fast at work conducting its War on Terror. Readers will have different views on the latter, but they can rest assured it won't be commented on here. It only rates mention in consideration of the administration release of Bush's "Blueprint for the American Dream" in the year after the war began. In a speech about the blueprint, Bush oddly tied home ownership to the war. In his own words, "Let me first talk about how to make sure America is secure from a group of killers. You know what they hate? They hate that somebody can go buy a home." Yes, you read that right. Having made a jejune case that it was "in our national interest that more people own their home," Bush ultimately defended tax credits and grants as a necessary part of the War on Terror.[16]

Ideally readers get the picture by now. In a policy sense, housing is the ultimate sacred cow in Washington. Other than perhaps food or education, nothing much comes close to home ownership as a vehicle for political posturing, and much worse, subsidy.

Which brings us to the title of our book: *Bringing Adam Smith into the American Home*. It emerged from a discussion the two of us had last year about housing. Jack Ryan suggested that Adam Smith needed to inform more of the housing discussion. Jack's assertion, seemingly made in offhanded fashion, was manna from heaven for John Tamny. Though our Zoom discussion (yes, we, too, found ourselves part of the Zoom culture in 2020) began as a phone conversation about op-ed writing, Jack's comment was the spark for a book idea.

Letting Adam Smith into the home is so important on so many levels. Smith, were he around today, would marvel at how much politicians have drunk the home-ownership Kool-Aid. As the quote that begins our introductory chapter makes plain, Smith was very clear in *The Wealth of Nations* that the purchase of a home was just that. It was in no real way an expander of commerce or knowledge. In fact, like every other important purchase, buying a home is merely a "buy versus lease" consumption decision, which should use the analysis nearly everyone has been taught in basic economics.

Put another way, when we as individuals purchase homes, we're not opening up foreign markets, we're not increasing our commercial efficiency, nor will our purchases lead to new communications, health, or transportation advances. When you buy a house, you do just that. Once we realize having a place to live is consumption, then we can move on to the real issues which are how to finance it, leasing it versus buying it, and then how to manage it.

However, the purchase of a home arguably limits the mobility of the buyer. This is important in consideration of Smith's views about the essential importance of human movement. Smith put the expansion of the capital base on a high pedestal in his economic hierarchy, after which it's no reach to say that that in the information age human beings are the ultimate capital. Particularly in modern times, home ownership is the proverbial ball and chain that holds down the very humans responsible for all economic progress.

As Adam Smith has written, every person should be able to reach his or her full potential and experience the flourishing of the human spirit. To achieve the apogee of this ideal, the process of becoming the best version of oneself should be as frictionless as possible. Being tied to a specific location with extremely high switching costs and transaction costs degrades human capital and the full potential of the individual. In addition, the mindshare that is consumed by thinking about managing an asset, or thinking about a skill, at which one is not expert is a huge burden to the individual who should be advancing their unique talents or consuming their leisure for those things that maximize their joy. Having to manage a complex home produces a deadweight loss to both society and the individual. It is in direct contrast to Smith's specialization of labor.

Through his pin factory example in *Wealth of Nations*, Smith artfully revealed the genius of labor divided, and the remarkable productivity that results from individuals doing what they do best. What's true in production is also true in living. Housing not only limits our movement to what elevates our best selves, it also forces us to ferociously despecialize by dint of owning a living space in the first place. Through the specialization of labor, all of us become very good at something such as lawyering, banking, car producing, or coding. And then we all trade with each other thereby maximizing each other's wealth. We should not be engaged in activities about which we know little, which thereby destroys our productivity, clouds our minds, and diminishes one of the most valuable of our assets: our leisure to enjoy our families, friends, and the world.

So why, in the twenty-first century, should Adam Smith be stopped at everyone's front door? In fact, he should be warmly invited in because very few of us, even individuals engaged full time in a specific trade, are expert at plumbing, carpentry, painting, generating power, or all the other skills it takes to maintain or improve a home. Adam Smith's insights of division and specialization of labor, which have permeated nearly all of every other human endeavor, are a distant theory inside the twenty-first century home. In fact, in the twenty-first century homeowners are still behaving as they did in the seventeenth century—when everyone raised their own crops, made their own clothes, manufactured their own barrels, and built and managed their own homes. Furthermore, with twenty-first century technology, a home is an asset that is getting increasingly more complex to manage every year.

Some reading this are doubtless shaking their heads. "Housing is a necessity like food. Human capital is nothing without the two." True enough. Housing is an essential market good. Without it, life would be primitive and defined by relentless drudgery. And if readers doubt our sincerity, they might change their tune if aware that Jack is the founder of REX, a full service residential real estate brokerage which depends on people owning, buying, and selling homes.

The book you're about to read isn't a polemic against housing as much as it's a call for reason. In the third decade of the twenty-first century as we write, housing has morphed from an essential human good into a capital-depleting barrier to frontierless human advance. As opposed to lifting humanity to a better state of being, we think the fundamental urge increasingly limits human progress. Imagine a contra-world in which it is virtually free to move about the country. What would happen to the spirit, wealth, and the ultimate potential of the individual and the economy?

In what is a short book, we will lay out for readers in plain English why American obsession with ownership has become a restraint on the ability of the American people (and people around the world) to reach a better place in terms of living and working standards. We will then show readers why home ownership may not be the best answer if the goal is progress.

Some might deduce from the previous paragraph that the reading in future chapters will include policy solutions meant to blunt the presumed "American Dream" of home ownership. Fear not. Paraphrasing another great economic observer Joseph Schumpeter, "We offer no policy."

What we instead seek is free markets, including free markets in the markets for the sale of homes. Sure enough, the cost of selling one's home exists as a major barrier to same. It's our view that free, unfettered competition in the real estate brokerage space would have a transformative impact on the economy precisely because it would make it easier to exit what Washington has strived mightily to make very easy to enter.

As we conclude our introduction, we will do so by making a basic point: consumption is the easy part. Figure that we all have endless wants, including wants for housing. Crucial about this is that consumption is the logical corollary of production. Stated another way, without production there quite simply is no consumption. We produce so that we can consume.

It's all a reminder that governments needn't ever worry about trying to stimulate consumption. It's what we're wired to do. More realistically, governmental attempts to stimulate consumption bring new meaning to superfluous, or worse, create market distortions that can ultimately result in catastrophe.

Rather than rely on government to subsidize and thus distort market forces for homes, a much better way for government to behave is to let real markets operate. When assets are liquid, there is less risk in acquiring them because they can be sold easily, and thus are purchased more readily. Liquid assets also have less price volatility than illiquid assets, and have shorter down periods thus limiting their price volatility. In this book and its afterword, we will also demonstrate how the cartelization of the realty industry restrains the productive and efficient work of Smith's invisible hand.

The above truth raises a basic question: Why, despite an American obsession with property, have U.S. politicians for so long found the need to subsidize the obsession? Americans already consume property with abandon, yet politicians routinely look for new ways to make our itch of an overwhelming scratch easier and easier.

That's where we'll start with chapter 1. Why the stimulation of so much consumption? And yes, housing *is* consumption.

# CHAPTER ONE

# Despite What They Tell You, Housing Is Not Investment

*"Capitals are increased by parsimony, and
diminished by prodigality and misconduct."*

– Adam Smith, *The Wealth of Nations*, p. 367

I t's very hard to contemplate in modern times, but in centuries past books were extraordinarily expensive. Call them the private jets of the medieval era. You laugh? Please read on.

As *Anathema!* author Marc Drogin explained it, "It is extremely difficult to report, in contemporary terms, and/or contemporary coin of the realm, the price of a medieval book." Needless to say, "surviving accounts of the value of books" rated mention because their costs were "so unusually high."[17]

While a Bible has long been easy to find in the bedside drawer of seemingly every hotel and motel room in the U.S.,

Drogin reports that "very few priests were known to possess Bibles." The cost of just one well exceeded a year's pay.

What about borrowing books? Libraries were far from a thing as evidenced by U.S. Steel industrialist Andrew Carnegie giving away millions in the twentieth century to found them for the public. Since people literally couldn't afford books, Carnegie would create libraries from which they could borrow them.

Of course, before the creation of all this capitalist plenty that led to public libraries, few were willing to part ways with something so rare as a book. Better yet, book owners inserted warnings inside what was remarkably rare:

"Whoever takes away this book, May he never on Christ look."[18]

While nowadays books are signed, in more primitive times those who opened books were treated to threats related to stealing what brought new meaning to scarce. Imagine that!

So what changed? Why are books everywhere today? Why are they so common and easy to attain that most can't be bothered to borrow them, or secure a library card in order to borrow them? The answer is economic growth.

Economic growth produces wealth, and when it's abundant, it produces surplus. The surplus is what's crucial to progress. While frequently misguided economists claim that consumption powers economic growth, the reality is quite different.

As the introductory chapter made plain, consumption is the easy part in a sense. We all have endless wants, and we produce so that we can fulfill those wants. Consumption is fun.

In truth, the real driver of progress is savings. It's the unspent wealth that propels us forward via investment. In Smith's words, every frugal man is a "public benefactor."[19] In other words, there are no entrepreneurs without capital. The savers are the most crucial players in human advance. Most economists have it backwards.

Looked at through the prism of books, it arguably began with Johannes Gutenberg. He brought to the world a mechanical moveable type printer that replaced handwritten books. And since the fifteenth century, books have become cheaper and cheaper with the advent of a "Printing Revolution" sparked by Gutenberg. Not only do many foundations funded by the rich (or their descendants) offer all manner of books for free, the simple truth is that the profit-motivated attained wealth by relentlessly developing ever more innovative ways to mass produce the former luxury that was the book. This is what happens when savings are matched with tinkerers. Through time their experimentation results in supply explosions of once scarce goods such that they make it easier and much cheaper to acquire what used to be nosebleed in a cost sense.

Figure that wealth is historical. While ownership of a "library" plainly signaled immense wealth in centuries past, nowadays all too many of us can claim cases and cases of books. That's why they so often sell for next to nothing (or nothing at all) in thrift shops. We're literally searching for takers of our excess.

Savings make it possible for entrepreneurs to rush a much more abundant future into the present. While it was once books, nowadays the entrepreneurial are feverishly working on ways to figuratively shrink the world. Companies like Boom Technology and Spike Aerospace are fast at work developing the next generation of air travel—travel that will be supersonic. In practical terms, six-hour flights from New York to London will soon enough take three and a half hours, and ten-hour flights from San Francisco to Tokyo will soon enough require six hours of plane time.[20] Boom and Spike hope to ferry actual passengers around by 2029, but the more intriguing concept is what air travel will be like in *2129*. What's certain is that the more individuals save over the next 100+ years, the more experimentation that will enable huge technological leaps.

Giant economic leaps rate discussion in concert with housing given the faulty view among all too many economists that housing vitality powers economic vitality. Quite the opposite, really. Housing is a consumptive consequence of economic advance despite what economists believe. To offer up an example of conventional housing thought that this book aims to correct, consider a 2008 *Wall Street Journal* opinion piece by Columbia Business School professors R. Glenn Hubbard and Christopher Mayer. Calling for federal intervention in the mortgage market in order to achieve mortgage-lending rates of 4.5 percent, Hubbard and Mayer claimed the then-lower rates would boost the housing market, thus sparking a broad economic boom. In their words, more expensive houses (for readers who've forgotten, the housing market had endured a bit of a correction a few months prior...) would "provide a housing wealth effect" that would subsequently "make consumers feel richer" on the way to a huge surge in consumption.[21] To economists, this is growth.

Looking back to 2008, is it any wonder the economic outlook had become so bleak? Hubbard had served George W. Bush as his chairman of the administration's Council of Economic Advisers, and it showed. Though gargantuan consumption of housing had ended in tears just months before, though government error had played a major role in the consumption (though not for the reasons you've been told to think), we had some of the world's most renowned economists calling for the federal government to double down on what had ended so badly not too long ago. You can't make this up!

Back to some semblance of reason, what we call an "economy" is not some living, breathing blob. An economy is *individuals*. Applied to a country, it's the citizenry. Nothing more, nothing less.

Thinking about what's simple when it comes to economy, it's much easier to see just how confused the economic models are that prevail today. Again, most economists aim for stimulation of consumption, including housing consumption, as the path to growth. In a 2020 opinion piece published amid immense optimism about the housing market, CNN economic and market analyst Paul La Monica wrote of housing as "an undeniable bright spot" that was "holding up" a U.S. economy that had been crushed to varying degrees by the lockdowns related to the coronavirus.[22] La Monica's modeling brought new meaning to shallow.

To see why, we need only consider the individuals that are the economy. Is the individual who consumes with abandon more prosperous? Better yet, *are you* better off economically if you blithely go from paycheck to paycheck without saving a cent? The question answers itself. The individual is most certainly improved by saving, and this proves particularly true when bad times reach the spendthrifts in our midst. In other words, jobless and without savings to fall back on is right up there on any meter of economic despair.

Important about all this is that the very abstinence that boosts the economy of the individual similarly lifts the overall economy. In Smith's words, while consumption is a certain spur to production, the wanton "purchasing" of goods for "home consumption" essentially "promotes prodigality" without "increasing production." Conversely, when we don't spend it's not as though our savings sit idle as much as what's unspent employs "an additional number of industrious people."[23] The unspent is what enables industrial progress.

Think yet again about formerly scarce books. Absent a lack of consumption there wouldn't have been the capital formation necessary for experimentation that enabled mass production. Production is what enables demand. *Always.*

More modernly, the eventual arrival of profitable, quiet, and clean supersonic flight (the Concorde provided none of the three) will greatly increase individual productivity precisely because it will increase the time available to business travelers to produce. Consumption is yet again a logical consequence of production, but it seems economists have forgotten that savings are what make it possible for the individuals in any economy to constantly increase their productivity. In short, savings to fund the innovator and to enhance productivity are an essential driver of higher progress, higher living standards, and, yes, exponentially greater production without which there is no consumption.

In other words, many in the economics profession have reversed causation. Consumption doesn't boost economic growth; rather, it's the consequence of it. Production first, then consumption.

Looked at through housing, as the introductory chapter made plain, the purchase of a house doesn't open foreign markets or enhance our skills on the job, it doesn't boost our productivity on the job, and it certainly doesn't expand capitalist plenty. Indeed, homeownership usually reduces all three by taking away time from each of the above. To see why, consider another industrial giant in Amazon. But to understand just one aspect of the multi-faceted retailer, it's useful to travel back in time to the relative drudgery that prevailed before the Seattle behemoth.

Back before the internet, and as recently as the 1980s and '90s, cars were largely sold by owners in newspapers. Owners purchased "classified" ad space in which they described what they had for sale. Hard as it is to imagine today, owners were very clear if the car had AM/FM radio, and if a tape deck was part of the car's technological package, this was prominently noted. It's puzzling now, but in the '80s and early '90s tape decks were still luxury items that rated mention. They signaled modernity. How things change. Really, as we write we're imagining more than a few readers wondering what actually a "tape deck" is!

The main thing is that, as previously noted, luxury is historical. Soon enough the certain luxury that was the CD player replaced the tape deck in cars. So coveted were these car stereos with CD players that owners of same not infrequently found themselves returning to their parked cars only to find out that the stereo had been stolen. Eventually car stereo manufacturers started producing models that could be removed from the car with ease. Yes, it used to be that people carried their car stereos with them after parking their cars on the street.

Of course, capitalist endeavor has rendered the tape deck a fossil of the past, and the CD player is just about there too. Nowadays, we can command music with our voices. CDs are so yesterday.

Indeed, ownership of an Amazon Echo enables purchase of a monthly subscription to Amazon Music. For $4.49, subscribers quite literally have something resembling all of the world's recorded music at their disposal. Just ask Alexa to play your favorite songs, and she will. Can't remember the name of the song? Is the tune's chorus all that you remember? It's no trouble. Alexa has been trained to know alternative names to seemingly every song under the sun. Even better, we nowadays can get Alexa in our cars. Yes, as we drive along, we have a multi-billion-dollar music collection at the tip of our tongues.

So how did we get here? How is it that former luxuries like the tape deck and CD have been so disdainfully placed in the proverbial museum of gadgets past? How can access to music that formerly would have cost billions now be had for $4.99 a month? By now, readers know the answer.

Progress is the reward for parsimony. When we don't consume our existing wealth and instead save, the unspent wealth frequently flows to those with an itch to produce a future that in no way resembles the present.

Amazon founder Jeff Bezos has by his own admission spent billions on failures. For instance, does anyone remember the Amazon Fire mobile phone? In Bezos's own words, "Failure comes part and parcel with invention." More important, Bezos and his colleagues *rush* to failure as a way of learning how to succeed. Bezos arguably puts it best: "We…believe in failing early and iterating until we get it right."[24]

Ok, but failing is expensive. Most see Silicon Valley-style companies like Amazon as the path to great wealth, but Bezos told his very own parents that Amazon's odds of failure were well over 70 percent.[25] Again, this is all very expensive, which speaks once again to the importance of savers.

When we don't spend, we can transfer our wealth to those seeking to multiply it. When we consume, that's it. A purchase of a house will not lead to the next Amazon in the way that the purchase of shares in a company aiming to replace Amazon's dominance might.

With savings, what we've not consumed frequently flows to entrepreneurs eager to create wealth that *doesn't yet exist*. When we consume, we're purchasing wealth and market goods that *already exist*.

Put housing in the category of wealth that *already exists*.

To be clear once again, housing is a *necessary* consumptive good. There's no arguing with this basic truth. But let's not pretend that consumption of housing is stimulative, that per Professors Hubbard and Mayer, and CNN's La Monica, that vibrant housing is the catalyst for massive industry. It quite simply is not. Housing is what we purchase after we've been industrious.

Per the Smith quote that kicks off the introductory chapter, the purchase of a house isn't a sign of the capital formation necessary for entrepreneurs to innovate, nor will "the revenue of the whole body of the people" be "in the smallest degree increased by it." Call housing a sink of wealth. A necessary one, but let's end right here the mythology that individual ownership of housing is just another investment class in the way that small caps, large cap value, and venture capital are.

Some of those reading are no doubt resisting what we're writing. "How can housing not be investment? The house I purchased in 1980, 1990, 2008, or 2019, has appreciated a great deal. It's been my best investment." The question is reasonable, but not specific enough. The question is: "My best investment relative to what?"

Did your investment in a home outpace the return on equities over that period, venture capital, or inflation-adjusted bonds? Moreover, have you fully allocated your own labor, maintenance costs, opportunity costs, and other yearly expenses against your return in maintaining your home to keep it appreciating? Furthermore, have you accrued for the real costs of your distracted mindshare while you think about an issue that has arisen in your home and what to do about it? Which mindshare might be better spent on topics in which you are expert? Additionally, have you thought about the price you pay for leisure, and accrued for the problems that distract your mind from your unfettered relaxation? To everyone, leisure is also an asset. Thinking about a depreciating refrigerator and your alternatives, much less working to remedy it, devalues that important asset.

Which is why the next chapter will focus on what stimulates housing consumption at the expense of investment. In advance, we'll hint that the low interest rates pointed to by the pundit class are not the housing consumption spur, or housing valuation enhancer that so many have become conditioned to believe.

In other words, we promised readers a different look at housing and its economic meaning, and we fully intend to deliver.

CHAPTER TWO

## Housing Consumption and the Low Interest Rate Myth

*"Ask any rich man of common prudence,*
*to which of the two sorts of people he has*
*lent the greater part of his stock, to those*
*who, he thinks, will employ it profitably,*
*or those who will spend it idly, and he will*
*laugh at you for proposing the question."*

– Adam Smith, *The Wealth of Nations*, p. 381

Alan Greenspan was out of government and in the private sector conducting the economic analysis that he'd long enjoyed. Still, he was worried. His concern was that his employees weren't being thorough enough in their own analysis. One of them, Kathryn Eickhoff, "had been telling clients that a hot housing market was driving consumer spending: people were taking out second mortgages on their homes and using the proceeds to remodel their kitchens or purchase new cars, turbocharging the economy."[26]

The empiricist in Greenspan was worried that Eickhoff's assertions weren't rooted in rigorous study. He felt she'd failed to "get the data" to prove her argument. No problem. Greenspan would conduct his own investigation of some kind of housing "wealth effect." What he found astonished him. In gathering up the numbers, he soon told Eickhoff that she "had absolutely no idea of the size of this phenomenon."[27]

Sure enough, mortgage issuance had exploded. It was six times the normal amount of the previous decade.[28] Housing prices had tripled.[29] Yes, it soon became apparent that the only error in Eickhoff's analysis was one of conservatism about how hot the housing sector was. Greenspan's research revealed just that.

Readers doubtless have an opinion here. Greenspan left the Fed on January 31, 2006, and as many remember, housing was most certainly hot at the time. Much more than hot. Seemingly everyone had a housing story of the buying and selling variety, and often both. It was the topic *du jour*. What's been reported is hardly news. Greenspan's research proved what everyone who was mildly sentient could see and hear with their eyes and ears in 2006.

Except that the occurrence you just read about didn't take place in 2006. It's a true story from *1977*. When Greenspan returned to private economic consulting after serving as chairman of the Council of Economic Advisers under President Gerald Ford.

So while Eickhoff's belief that housing consumption would drive economic growth was as wrongheaded in the 1970s as it was in the 2000s, her research is yet another reminder that the Fed's low-rate policies had little to do with the housing boom that took place in the twenty-first century. We know this because the Fed's funds rate was soaring in the '70s. This is important mainly because it's long been accepted wisdom that the Fed's "easy money," low-rate targets were the source of the much-chronicled housing boom of the 2000s that ended somewhat gruesomely in 2008. What Greenspan saw in the '70s will hopefully cause readers to rethink what's never made much sense. What's never made sense is that housing attains vitality from low rates of interest.

To be clear, housing roared upward in the 1970s when the Fed was *aggressively hiking rates*. The conventional view that the central bank can engineer rushes to real estate has little basis.

As a way of underscoring what happened in the '70s, it's useful now to turn to futurist George Gilder on the matter. Gilder, in his recall of the '70s housing boom, noted in his 1981 book *Wealth and Poverty* that "what happened was that citizens speculated on their homes… Not only did their houses tend to rise in value about 20 percent faster than the price index, but with their small equity exposure they could gain higher percentage returns than all the but the most phenomenally lucky shareholders."[30] Gilder added that,

> While 24 million investors in the stock market were being buffeted by inflation and taxes, 46 million homeowners were leveraging their houses with mortgages, deducting the interest

payments on their taxes, and earning higher real returns on their down payment equity than speculators in gold or foreign currencies. Then they parlayed their gains into second mortgages to be spent on durable goods – the washers and storm windows, color televisions and automobiles – that they would use for their retreat from the perils of money in inflationary America.

By 1979 the value of individually owned dwellings had reached 1.3 trillion dollars, twice the value of individually owned corporate stock.[31]

The main thing is that if Greenspan's experience with a soaring housing market in the '70s alongside Gilder's recollection doesn't open some eyes, it's hard to know what will. At the very least it's fair to contend that if readers were presented with Greenspan and Gilder's findings as though they'd been written in 2006, no honest person would bat an eye. The parallels are eerie, yet the Fed was once again aggressively hiking its rate target in the '70s as opposed to pushing it to 1 percent in the early 2000s.

In short, the '70s reveal popular arguments about the Fed's role in the rush to housing of the 2000s as much more than wanting. Not only does consumption of housing shrink economic growth (the latter the principal flaw in the Eickhoff-Greenspan thesis which said housing consumption was a stimulant), it soars for reasons unrelated to the central bank's rate target.

At which point it's worth it now to digress—only slightly—into money. Don't worry, this will be brief. Up front, no one borrows money, lends it, pays it, or earns it.

Underlying all monetary exchanges is production, or the exchange of production. Money isn't wealth as much as it's an agreement about value that makes it much easier for actual wealth to change hands. A foot measures length; money measures value.

In that case, money is as old as trade is among humans. It's what enabled the specialization of labor which Adam Smith proves creates real wealth. If there was a fixed agreement about value among producers, they could comfortably trade the surplus from their production in order to get what they weren't producing.

Reduced to the basics, the butcher longingly eyes the brewer's beer, but the brewer only wants the baker's bread. A common measure of value (money) facilitates exchange among these producers who have different tastes and needs. Arguably the most quoted line of all in *The Wealth of Nations* is Smith's observation that "it is not from the benevolence of the butcher, the brewer, or the baker, that we expect our dinner, but from their regard for their own interest."[32] Truer words have rarely been written. As economic actors we produce out of self-interest, we produce in order "to get," as producers we're "importers," but our ability to import is greatly enhanced the more that our own work or production is specialized. When we're doing what animates our talents, we're much more productive. Very importantly, credible money assuredly facilitates the specialization. If money is trusted as a measure of exchangeable value, the butcher can comfortably hand over a large cut of meat to a brewer offering money given knowledge that he'll be able to attain bread equal in value to his meat from the baker with the money handed to him by the brewer.

With trade it's always products for products. Money is just the referee. In the words of Smith, "The sole use of money is to circulate consumable goods."[33] Good money enables relentless trade among producers, and by extension, specialization.

Hopefully this digression into money makes it plain for readers that when we borrow dollars, we're borrowing access to real resources—*to actual market goods*. When we're lending dollars, we're lending near-term access to real resources. When we pay or we're paid, we're transferring or taking in access to market goods. When we transfer money to others in a market-place, or have it transferred to us, there's a cost or interest rate associated with it given the basic truth that money is a claim on wealth in the marketplace. When we borrow money, we're attaining near-term access to goods and services that someone else is giving up in return for greater access (thus the interest rate) down the line.

The aside about money will hopefully provide readers with a practical understanding of why the popular view about low Fed interest rates driving the housing vitality never made sense. Forget that the 1970s seriously call into question the thesis, and just consider the practicality of the narrative.

It's long implied that the Fed could make access to resources cheap just by decreeing it so. By that bit of illogic, the mayors of notoriously expensive cities like Hong Kong, London, and New York could make apartments cheap just by declaring them to be, or legally mandating that they be inexpensive. Lots of luck there. Any artificializing of apartment rents on the low side would render demand for "easy" apartments high, but supply of new apartments low, thereby doing the *opposite of what the mayors intend.*

Implicit in the view that the Fed made credit "easy" in the 2000s on the way to a housing boom was that the Fed could decree access to the claim on wealth that is money "cheap," or 1 percent, and that those with money to loan (sellers) would comply. The very notion defies basic common sense. If there's such thing as "easy money," the latter implies that there's easy access to market goods, services, materials, and so on. In other words, the Fed couldn't make money "easy" even if it wanted to. The cost of accessing dollars is set in the marketplace, and it's rarely cheap.

That is so because there are always more bidders for market goods, services, and materials than there is supply. Jack knows this well from his days at Goldman Sachs. Investment bankers aren't paid extraordinarily well because access to credit is cheap; they're rightly paid handsomely precisely because credit is very hard to attain. And it's difficult to attain because compound interest is easily the most powerful force in all of investing. To pretend that the Fed can make credit "easy" by decreeing it so is to pretend that those with title to wealth will forego the remarkable compound genius of having that title whenever the Fed essentially decides they should give away the abundant fruits of compounding for nothing. Popular views about the Fed are much less than serious.

In which case, you the reader can insouciantly ask why, assuming abundant credit, that it would flow to housing as has long been assumed. The very idea vandalizes common sense.

As the previous chapter makes plain, housing is not investment. It's consumption. A purchase of a house won't multiply wealth as much as it's at best a store of wealth. Which is why the thesis about "low" rates decreed by the Fed as the spark that lit the housing boom of the 2000s is just so trite and silly. In the words of Smith, "Whenever a great deal can be made by the use of money, a great deal will commonly be given for the use of it."[34] Translating Smith for those who need it, in any economy there are always myriad bidders for access to precious resources. Housing would never—in a normal scenario—be able to attract lending at near zero rates when there's so much demand for resources at higher rates.

In other words, "money" logically flows to its most remunerative use as the Smith quote from the previous paragraph makes plain—meaning not housing. Indeed, the returns on property just aren't that great relative to, for instance, the stock market. As Niall Ferguson calculated it in *The Ascent of Money*, $100,000 invested in the U.S. property market in 1987 had tripled in value by 2007, the theoretical high-water mark of the 2000s' housing boom. Conversely, that same $100,000 invested in the S&P 500 Index from '87 rose to $772,000 by 2007.[35] About Ferguson's calculations, it's worth keeping in mind that the stock-market timeframe includes the biggest U.S. equity crash in history; 1987's gruesome 22.5 percent decline on October 19, 1987. Despite this, an investment in a broad U.S. equity index brought you much greater wealth gains than did home ownership.

Which leads to an obvious question: Why housing? If it's not an investment, and if it doesn't perform as investments in the stock market normally do, why the flow of precious wealth into the housing sector in the first place?

The simple answer up front is one that's been touched on from the outset: housing is an essential market good. *We must have shelter.* While not an investment per se, housing is theoretically a form of saving that we can live in. As individuals we're willing to borrow money in the form of a mortgage so that we have a place to live, and our monthly mortgage payments gradually expand our ownership of the house.

It's also worth keeping in mind that far from a risky investment, housing is relatively safe. While something on the order of 90 percent of Silicon Valley-style businesses fail, the default rate for mortgages is very low.[36] This was even true during the early 2000s housing boom. Though it's popular to imagine a housing collapse of enormous proportions due to junky mortgages, the actual default rate for mortgages issued during the frothy, manic 2004–2008 period was something less than 10 percent.[37]

Housing is once again safe. When a business fails, its most crucial "assets" (people) are released to better opportunities elsewhere. This isn't true with housing. When owners can no longer keep current on mortgage payments, the market good underlying the mortgage payment (the house) is recoverable. While an equity investor in a business loses his investment when a promising business goes belly-up, those who go belly-up on mortgages don't exactly leave their lenders high and dry. They instead release a physical house to the lenders.

That housing is relatively safe speaks to why voluminous amounts of wealth flows to home loans. Those with savings to varying degrees want to avoid exposing all of their wealth to riskier forms of investment. A purchase of public shares in the stock market brings obvious risk. Again, if the company goes under, an investor has no claims on what's left over. Same with an investor in private shares of a potential tech "unicorn." Stocks and venture capital investments return more than do housing purchases precisely because they're riskier. Investments in mortgages provide relatively safe access to income streams for savers who desire a more stable, more certain return on their wealth.

Yet during certain periods housing seems to attract a greater amount of savings than normal. As this chapter has shown, the 1970s and 2000s are two very prominent examples from fairly modern times. What explains surges of willingness among savers to enable housing consumption? Unsurprisingly, Smith answered the question. As he explained it, "It would be too ridiculous to go about seriously to prove, that wealth does not consist in money, or in gold and silver; but in what money purchases, and is valuable only for purchasing."[38]

Smith was clarifying on his simple assertion about money. It's not wealth. It facilitates the exchange of wealth. Money is an agreement about value that is a claim on wealth, as opposed to money on its own having some kind of tangible value. Money's value is, per Smith, in what "money purchases, and is valuable only for purchasing." Money is once again a measure. Always keep this in mind.

As individuals we produce in order to get things, but sometimes we delay our consumption. Readers are already familiar with this from the previous chapter. What we don't spend is essentially rented to others in the marketplace. Savers are "public benefactors" in Smith's analysis, because what they don't spend builds up a capital base that entrepreneurs and businesses can draw on in order to purchase the resources necessary to turn a concept into an industrial reality. Savings are what make progress possible. We measure our savings in money.

Of course, sometimes monetary authorities devalue the money that we've acquired and that exists as a store of wealth for us. If per Smith money's value is a consequence of what the "money purchases," devaluation shrinks what money can purchase. Devaluation shrinks the measure. That it does has obvious market implications. And surely implications for savers.

To see why, consider what an investor is buying when he puts wealth to work through purchase of public or private shares. Very specifically the investor is buying future returns in *money*. In a U.S. sense, an investor in American companics is buying future returns in dollars.

All of which speaks to why currency devaluation is such an investment deterrent. Why put wealth to work if any far-from-certain returns are going to come back in shrunken dollars? Call devaluation a tax on investment.

When we invest, we're speculating on what could be wealth in the future if our capital commitments bear fruit. This is no easy feat. The future is rather opaque. As Jack knows so well, all too many companies (whether public or private) that seem attractive today won't be so attractive tomorrow, a year from now, or ten years from now. Dynamic economies have a way of rapidly turning today's hot commercial concept into tomorrow's afterthought.

Looked at through the prism of devaluation again, if a currency is in decline there's a greater tendency to take risk off of the table in order to purchase wealth that already exists. Housing is just that. While a Silicon Valley start-up has extraordinarily high odds of vanishing in short order, houses realistically last for centuries. Call them an inflation hedge, or a rush away from risk. They're really one and the same. When currency devaluation makes speculation on future wealth creation too risky, savings are more likely to flow into what's already wealth.

This very capably explains a rush into housing in the '70s and 2000s that was enabled by more expansive access to mortgages. The dollar was devalued in both decades. This was the policy of both decades. When President Nixon severed the dollar's long-time link to gold (the dollar was 1/35th of a gold ounce from 1933–1971) in 1971, the latter was an explicit admission that U.S. dollar policy favored devaluation. Markets complied. The dollar plummeted. What used to purchase 1/35th of a gold ounce in 1970 was exchangeable for 1/450th of a gold ounce a decade later.

In the 2000s, the dollar purchased roughly 1/275th of a gold ounce in 2000. During George W. Bush's presidency, the expressed dollar policy from the Bush Treasury favored devaluation. By 2008 the dollar was exchangeable for something less than 1/870th of a gold ounce. About these numbers, some may ask why gold as a measure? Simply put, gold tells the truth. Without getting into the good or bad of a gold standard, there's a reason central banks and monetary authorities to this day maintain so much in the way of gold holdings. Precisely because it has such few uses, and precisely because it's never consumed, it's *nonpareil* as a measure of money. That's why Smith references it throughout *The Wealth of Nations*. Its stability renders it better as money or as a definer of money than anything else market actors have come up with over time.

Crucial about gold is that its surge in dollars in the '70s and 2000s signaled a decline in the value of the dollar. A substantial one. Credit is never "easy," but with dollar devaluation rendering investment in the creation of future wealth far less certain, existing wealth, think "hard assets," received a lot more attention. In the words of political commentator David Frum in his dazzling book about the slow-growth 1970s, *How We Got Here*, back then, "If you had the nerve to borrow a lot of soggy cash, and then use it buy hard assets – land, grain, metals, art, silver candlesticks, a book of Austro-Hungarian postage stamps – you could make a killing." Notable here is that as savings preferences changed, so did the origin of wealth. When money is losing value, commodities like housing, oil, and gold that represent existing wealth tend to outperform. This showed up in wealth tables. Per Frum, in the first *Forbes 400* published in 1982, 153 members had fortunes related to real estate or oil. By 1998, after a major dollar recovery in the '80s and '90s, only 57 of the *Forbes* fortunes were real estate or oil-based.[39]

Repetition is useful when introducing readers to a perhaps new way of looking at things, and applied to housing, existing wealth prospers during periods of currency weakness. In Frum's words, with the dollar "melting away" in the '70s,[40] housing well outperformed as savings migrated from future concepts to relative safety in what was already established as "real" wealth. For added clarity, imagine if they shrunk the length of the foot to six inches. Most of us would suddenly be ten to twelve feet tall without our actual height changing one bit. With housing, shrinkage of the money measure frequently renders the house more valuable in the measure, but without changing the house's true value.

Interest rates don't drive housing vitality, but currency debasement often does. Call housing an inflation hedge the health of which can often improve when overall economic vitality is in decline. In other words, it's no surprise that housing has done so well in periods when equity markets have faltered a la the '70s and 2000s.

When money is being devalued, there's a flight to safety. *To consumption.* Why save dollars that are in decline? A soaring housing market is often a sign of investors taking risk off of the table in order to expose their wealth to surer things. There's a certain quality to housing that a stock certificate doesn't provide.

More broadly, always keep top of mind what Adam Smith meant about money flows. They signal movement of real resources. After which, the growth story (or lack thereof) is in the details. Good money associates with investment. With progress. Bad, devalued money associates with consumption, including housing that is least vulnerable to devaluation.

So while housing is undeniably an essential market good, periods of immense "investor" excitement about housing frequently signal something amiss. Indeed, savers are society's "public benefactors," but there's less incentive to save and provide capital in pursuit of future returns if devaluation will tax away their value. Hence housing.

Unfortunately, the problems with a rush into housing don't end there. The clue to the previous assertion comes from Smith's observation that "whenever a great deal can be made by the use of money, a great deal will commonly be given for the use of it." That money endlessly migrates to its highest use is the surest signal that people are, in a perfect world, migrating to where their skills can be best deployed. Except that housing can be an anchor delaying this migration.

# CHAPTER THREE

# That Which Holds People in Place Restrains Economic Progress

*"…land is a subject which cannot be*
*removed, whereas stock easily may. The*
*proprietor of land is necessarily a citizen of*
*the particular country in which his estate*
*lies. The proprietor of stock is properly a*
*citizen of the world, and is not necessarily*
*attached to any particular country."*

– Adam Smith, *The Wealth of Nations*, p. 914

"Our hearts just broke – they just wanted to get out of their lives," but "we had to drive off with Charlie and me hanging off the car literally beating the guys away."[41] Those are the words of Mike Martin about midway through *Crossing the Congo: Over Land and Water in a Hard Place*, the fascinating book he wrote with Chloe Baker (introduction) and Charlie Hatch-Barnwell (photos) about the trio's perilous 2013 drive across the Democratic Republic of Congo (DRC), from Kinshasa to South Sudan.

For those who think they know poverty, dysfunction, or basic corruption within government officialdom, they would be wise to pick up this essential book. Odds are they'll never view—or discuss—the three in the same way again. What the authors of *Crossing* report from the DRC brings new meaning to all three, and much, much more.

There's really no way to adequately retell what the authors witnessed, nor what they endured. Their journey into—and through—hell defies literary or photographic description.

Needless to say, readers of what aims to be a much happier book would do best to simply try and imagine beginning a drive from, for instance, Houston to Dallas, only for I-45 to be mostly unpaved, and mostly undrivable due to massive potholes everywhere along the route. The travelers would have to endure regular interruptions in their journey thanks to I-45 intermittently ending, the lulls in what no westerner would describe as an "interstate" littered with massive trees and smaller rivers that need to be cleared or crossed on manmade rafts sturdy enough to carry an automobile. And that's the just the beginning.

For the trip from Houston to Dallas to even passably resemble what the authors experienced in the DRC, there would have to be no signs indicating the exact direction to Dallas, and then if eager to attain guidance, every request would be met with outstretched hands from people loitering on the route, and who also treat the roadway as their personal toilet. There would be no internet or phone during the drive for GPS or calls for directions, access to mere buckets of water would have to be negotiated, food largely scarce, and then police, if at all helpful while most often drunk and stoned, would erect checkpoints throughout the route from which they'd try to shake down the well-to-do with bribes in return for information and passage.[42]

The above is a rather incomplete, G-rated description of what the authors endured over nearly 2,500 miles. While the average first-world driver can complete a 100-mile trip easily within ninety minutes, in the DRC, 100 miles traveled represents a very successful *day*. Figure that the authors' 710-mile passage from Kinshasa to Kananga alone took place over fifteen days. During one 5-mile stretch as they exited Kinshasa, they were stopped by government officials no less than four times.[43] So while even the cruel wouldn't wish a drive across the DRC on their worst enemies, the authors did it, by choice, mostly because "people said that it could not be done. That it was impossible."[44]

Such is life in a nation like the DRC that is, in the words of Martin, "one of the most bureaucratic, officious and corrupt countries in the world."[45] Merely getting from Point A to Point B is a nightmare, not to mention trying to cross a country so bereft of quality roads and road signs, but full of long-fingered police and people eager to make every mile of driving a trial. No wonder so many of the country's citizens want to get out.

Indeed, as Baker puts it early on, "The people we met all shared the same dream," which was getting to the West.[46] As Martin later explains, those who live in the hell that is the DRC view the West as "a paradise with endless luxuries and wealth."[47] They are correct. And there are so many reasons why they're correct. Books could be written, and have been about the correlation between free people, rule of law, free markets, and abundant wealth. We don't aim to expand or improve on what's already been written.

Instead, we will point to a perhaps unsung reason that a country like the United States is so incredibly prosperous. Think mobility.

In the U.S., opportunity and prosperity are never far away. Even better, the prosperity that's never far away is also never difficult to reach. Though pundits who should know better routinely complain about its "crumbling infrastructure," the reality is that the U.S.'s forty-eight states (Hawaii separated by a big stretch of the Pacific Ocean, Alaska similarly not connected geographically to the "lower 48") are wondrously connected, and easily drivable.

While it took Martin et al sixty days to drive 2,494 miles across the Congo, New York to Los Angeles is eminently doable within three days. Sans pockmarked roads, sans breaks in roads that require the creation of sturdy rafts, sans "checkpoints" manned by wasted police seeking "tribute," and sans danger.

Economic growth is a consequence of the relentless movement of resources to their highest use, and the greatest resource of all is human. In the U.S., people are free to move about this vast country without any restraints. What's impossible in the Congo is exceedingly easy here; the only question we face here is one of how we get around. Will it be by car, train, airplane, bike, or even foot? Figure that the U.S. has been traversed in all ways mentioned.

Stop and think about this for a minute. Maybe more. We hear all the time about the sources of U.S. prosperity: relatively light taxation and regulation, a dollar that is broadly trusted, deep capital markets, economic freedom that isn't of the Singapore kind, but close. Basically the U.S. is one big Singapore, in an economic sense.

But arguably the biggest driver of immense American prosperity is that there are no restraints on our movement. And other than technological limitations from the past, there never have been restraints foisted upon us.

As a free people, we've always been able to "take our talents" where they were most likely to be realized. Alexis de Tocqueville observed about Americans in the nineteenth century that they were "restless amid abundance."[48] Indeed, they were and *we are*.

Figure that we descend from people who had the drive and courage to leave all that they knew behind, only to risk their lives crossing oceans and borders in order to taste personal and economic freedom. Americans aren't a race as much as they're an ideal. Sorry, but we're different.

And as descendants of people who were on the move, so are we. Travel to most any U.S. state, and in particular cities and states with booming economies, and you'll routinely see voluminous out-of-state plates.

Jack in particular knows this well. An Illinoisan by upbringing, Jack's start-up, REX, is based in Austin, Texas, which is presently a "melting pot" within the melting pot that is the United States. According to Lawrence Wright, author of the 2018 book *God Save Texas*, no less than eight Californians move to Austin each day.[49]

It's also the American design. Though the founders envisioned rather autonomous U.S. states so that the American people could essentially choose their bliss in a governmental sense, their vision was for movement within the states to be completely free. In a trade sense within the U.S. the founders' Commerce Clause was written to make trade among people within the states very "regular." Put another way, there would be no barriers to exchange erected by, for instance, Massachusetts to goods produced in New York. The U.S. was founded as a zone of free trade. The latter cannot be minimized.

In thinking about the free flow of goods, it's perfectly reasonable to observe that the latter ensures daily raises for those who live and work within such a zone. When goods can flow freely, whether within countries or between countries, workers benefit from a bigger number of producers competing to serve their needs. That's the "daily raise," and it's brilliant. But increasingly inexpensive goods and services don't represent the greatest benefit of open markets, or free trade.

What recommends free exchange or trade the most is that it frees us to do the work that most elevates our unique talents. Work divided or the division of labor is by the very phrasing the way that humans migrate to the work that most enables their specialization. And when we're specialized in what we're doing, we logically produce quite a bit more. Arguably the second most referenced aspect of *The Wealth of Nations* is Smith's discussion of the pin factory he observed up close, and that is part of the book's opening. In Smith's words, "The greatest improvement in the productive powers of labour, and the greater part of their skill, dexterity and judgement with which it is anywhere directed, or applied, seem to have been the effects of the division of labour."[50]

From there, Smith famously describes the rather basic (at least in modern times) pin factory. He found that ten men pursuing their specialty in the manufacture of pins could together, through this division of labor, make up to 48,000 pins per day. At the same time, he observed that if these ten men had worked independently, "they certainly not each of them have made twenty, perhaps not one pin a day."[51] Again, specialized individuals are very productive individuals.

Which speaks loudly to why the U.S. has been so remarkably prosperous. Though its states would be autonomous in a policy sense (this has changed in modern times, but that's another story, or book), goods would flow seamlessly across state lines. Yes, in a country stretching from New York to California, the people across the country would get to divide up work with each other.

Arguably even better, the people freely exchanging goods and services, and dividing up work, would be free to move to where they could most specialize. And they did. See de Tocqueville and the U.S. now. Introduce yourself to most anyone in most any vibrant American city, and the question of "Where are you from?" nearly always comes up. Quite unlike the DRC where tragically awful roads are but one of many barriers to human mobility, in the U.S., the barriers to movement are largely within our own heads.

"Hit 'em where they ain't" was famously uttered by baseball legend Willie Keeler as the secret to hitting success. In the U.S., the secret is similarly basic: go to where the jobs are, or where opportunity is greatest, or where *you'll be greatest.* There are no limits. If opportunity is slight where you live, get up and go. Odds are your ancestors migrated against exponentially more challenging odds.

So while it's certainly true that mobility can—and routinely does—elevate restless, impatient Americans, there are barriers. We believe housing is one of them.

As has been previously mentioned, it's surely an essential market good. We all need shelter. And while home ownership isn't investment, it's a way to build up equity in what has modernly existed as an inflation hedge.

Still, ownership has its drawbacks. Ownership of property quite simply makes us less mobile. The great Canadian economist Reuven Brenner reminds us that the French refer to housing as *"immobilier."*[52] Home ownership ties us down.

Politicians in a sense love it because if we're tied to a house, or a specific location, we're easier to tax. It's kind of basic. *Immobilier* is wondrous for the political class. They can increase taxes dramatically as long as people can't move. The pessimistic among us might speculate that a not insignificant driver of the political class's reverence for home ownership isn't all the feel-good stuff about ownership society, but instead is rooted in the cynical realization that those immobilized by home ownership are easier to tax.

It's a reminder from the previous chapter that it would be unwise to consider home ownership solely as an inflation hedge, a way to save, but most of all as an "asset" relative to public equities. Such an approach arguably misses the point.

No doubt it's true that particularly over long stretches, stocks outperform housing. But the story is bigger than that. Stated simply, people arguably perform better the less that they are tied down. If not immobilized by ownership of a home, they're better positioned to migrate their talents to their greatest use in the quickest way possible.

If work divided drives specialization, and it does, then mobility of humans dividing up work lends itself to even greater specialization. We can seamlessly take our talents to their highest use when our savings are denominated in stocks, as opposed to property.

When we tie our wealth up in property, we're per Smith citizens of a particular state or country. Conversely, when our wealth is in equities, or bonds, we're realistically citizens of the world. Nothing holds us back.

The U.S.'s unsung genius has long arguably been ease of movement, we're still mobile for sure, but it's worth considering the unseen after decades of efforts by politicians to sanctify the alleged genius of home ownership. It's arguable that we're less mobile than we otherwise would be, to our individual detriment. The sacred cow that housing has become in a political sense has plainly drowned out Adam Smith's more reasonable view that what limits our movement, restrains our progress. Sorry, but home ownership is an embrace of a stationary state.

And the story doesn't end there. It's about more than government. The agency aspect of the housing industry is very much working against the best interests of home buyers and owners. In the next chapter, we'll explore efforts by the U.S. realty industry that place a huge tax on human migration above and beyond housing's immobilizing qualities.

# CHAPTER FOUR

# The NAR Cartel's Obnoxious Tax on Progress

*"The most decisive mark of the prosperity of any country is the increase of the number of its inhabitants."*

– Adam Smith, *The Wealth of Nations*, p. 80

"About the only thing German about Hoechst AG these days is its hard-to-pronounce name." Those were the words of *Wall Street Journal* reporters Greg Steinmetz and Matt Marshall way back in 1997. Germany the country could lay claim to many more than a few highly prominent corporations, but those same corporations were increasingly locating operations in countries *not* Germany.

In Hoecht's case its German workforce had declined to 45,000 from 80,000 such that only 30 percent of its employees worked in the "home country." What happened?

For one, it became expensive to hire in Germany. As Steinmetz and Marshall explained it, "German workers are the highest-paid, most pampered on earth." Their benefits generally included an extra month of pay at Christmas, six weeks of vacation per year, generous sick days that employees were known to take advantage of such that Germany had acquired the descriptive "The Lazy Man of Europe," plus when they were working the unions had negotiated average hourly pay of thirty dollars compared to seventeen dollars in the U.S.

It was quite simply difficult to hire in Germany because the costs of doing so were so steep. The story gets worse. Employees don't always live up to expectations. This was particularly problematic for German employers. Though average hourly pay was near double that of the U.S., strenuous labor laws made firing extraordinarily expensive. According to Steinmetz and Marshall, layoffs cost "five to 10 times as much" as they did in the U.S.

The story in France was similar. "I think the status of unemployed French people is often a great deal more enviable than the status of American workers." So said Jacques Attali in 1996. Attali had served at the highest of levels in French government. Attali was correct, in a sense. No doubt French workers in the late '90s could claim quite a bit of pampering in ways that German workers similarly could, but that Americans couldn't. Which was the point.

Just as in Germany, French employees were extraordinarily expensive to fire. Getting more specific, an employee who collected two paychecks would cost the business three to twelve months' worth of pay if let go. Maternity leave in France was gold plated too, not to mention that businesses were required to keep open for three years a job made vacant by a female on maternity leave. All these rules made hiring a pricey fool's errand such that in 1998, unemployment for French men and women under twenty-five was 22 percent.[53]

It's all a reminder that while governments and unions can negotiate all manner of benefits, impressive pay, and gold-plated dismissals, their demands are all for naught if the potential buyers find them to be too steep. They certainly did in France and Germany. In 1997, when Steinmetz and Marshall penned their front-page article, Germany had a rate of unemployment that was 12.2 percent.[54]

Stating what should be obvious, in certain countries there's an enormous tax levied on the hiring *and* firing of workers. Because there is, fewer workers are employed; that, or fewer workers are employed above the table. It's too costly.

German and French hiring practices in the late twentieth century are a good jumping off point toward the discussion of housing sales in the United States. The National Association of Realtors (NAR) is a powerful organization, and one that has worked successfully (at least for realtors…in theory) when it's come to keeping commissions on the sales of homes abnormally high. Lavish commissions have long existed as a major tax on the buying and selling of houses, which means they've existed as a tax on the very mobility that plays such an important role in capitalist prosperity rooted in, among other things, the relentless movement of capital and people to their highest use.

Adam Smith made plain as the chapter's opening quote indicates that prosperity's "decisive" mark is the "increase in the number of inhabitants." This is particularly true when it comes to individuals whose skills are highly desired within the marketplace. At risk of being blunt, the well-paid are huge job creators. Where they work is, per University of California-Berkeley professor Enrico Moretti, where job opportunity is most abundant. Considering Facebook alone, Moretti notes that its economic impact can't be limited to its employees. As he pointed out in his 2012 book *The New Geography of Jobs*, when thinking about the social media giant we must consider the tens of thousands of jobs created for Facebook apps, not to mention "at least 130,000 more jobs in related business services."[55]

The same applies to Apple. The focus can't just be on those entering its Cupertino headquarters each day. Moretti finds that similar to Facebook, there are tens of thousands of jobs related to Apple. As Moretti states so clearly, "In Silicon Valley, high-tech jobs are the *cause* of local prosperity, and the doctors, lawyers, roofers, and yoga teachers are the *effect*."[56]

The logic here is pretty intuitive when you think about it. The rich have myriad needs in addition to employees to staff their various ventures: they require investment banking and legal services, portfolio managers to help them put their wealth to work, plus they need hairstylists, dog walkers, personal trainers, and so on.

All of this speaks yet again to the importance of the mobility necessary to migrate one's talents to where opportunity is greatest. Those who are tied down the least are most able to get to where they can most showcase and get paid for their productive genius.

This simple truth first calls into question the various subsidies discussed in the introductory chapter, and that have been used by politicians over the decades to encourage home ownership. Housing is the "fourth rail" as it were to Social Security's third. Politicians go to great lengths in order to foster an ownership society, but it's hard to pair ownership of a consumptive good that to varying degrees immobilizes us with broad prosperity that is so directly tied to our individual ability to seamlessly migrate to the best work options. Stated simply, there's quite a bit more opportunity, and exponentially more varied opportunity, in Austin, Boston, and San Francisco relative to Aliquippa, Detroit, and Flint. Yet housing subsidies encourage us to stay put.

Artificial, highly inflated commissions to buy or sell a home double down on making people immobile. Consider the purchase of a $500,000 house. Commissions are earned by the buyer's realtor, but also that of the seller. Those commissions are usually in the 3 percent range for each side. At which point, let's do the basic math. On a $500,000 sale commissions add up to $30,000, which works out to roughly half of the median U.S. income. Jack knows this well. One could reasonably say intimately! Indeed, REX emerged from Jack's view that commissions charged by traditional realtors were way too high in consideration of the service provided by realtors. REX presently charges 2 to 2.5 percent commissions, headed to 0, on housing sales, while offering a much higher level of service.

More on commissions for housing sales in a bit.

For now, it's important to travel back in time yet again to the second half of the 1990s. Jack was a partner at Goldman

Sachs, and John was in the process of receiving his MBA at Vanderbilt's Owen Graduate School of Management. The location of John's graduate education is notable simply because at the time of his arrival, a professor at Owen (William G. Christie) was in the process of sleuthing a system of what we'll refer to as "courteous" pricing among equity traders.

Christie and Notre Dame professor Paul Schultz discovered that particularly on the NASDAQ market, equity prices rarely traded in "eighths." As Jack described it in a 2020 column for *RealClearMarkets*, "Stocks were never priced at eighths. Instead of pricing at the more accurate $20.125, for example, a stock was priced at $20.25."[57]

What Jack has referred to as "professionalism" gradually pervaded equity trading. Newbies to the business quickly learned that it was the opposite of courteous to trade in eighths. At which point an unspoken agreement made its way into a competitive industry that was arguably rendered less so. If the bid/ask spreads were wider than an eighth, trading profits would be greater for the traders, but at the expense of investors for whom buying and selling shares would be more expensive.

Christie and Schultz ultimately exposed the practice. About what they exposed, there are arguments that their findings were to some degree less than met the eye. To see why, consider buying a car with a plan to quickly flip it to another owner, versus buying one thousand shares in Amazon. With a car, a much-coveted model might sell right away while one that's more pedestrian could take weeks, and perhaps months to find a buyer. With blue chip equities there's a liquid market basically operating 24/7 such that there's generally always a buyer and a price to be had for one's shares. With cars, that's not always the case, at which point there's some risk associated with "holding" a car in a market that's not always liquid.

Looked at through the prism of equities, the market for Amazon shares is much more active than the one was and is for less known public companies. There was an argument in 1996, and there is one now, that it wasn't just courtesy or "professionalism" at work with equity spreads—that the risk associated with trading certain companies was paid back in wider spreads. John, who arrived at Goldman Sachs in 1997 as a new associate in the firm's equities division, takes the latter view. Either way, we both agree that any scenario that raises the cost of the buying and selling of any market good potentially shrinks the market.

How this played out in equities is that a deregulation of commissions that began in the 1970s continued with the discovery of Christie and Schultz. There was a running joke in the '70s that a stockbroker could leave for lunch as is, and come back well-to-do all based on commissions from one purchase order for shares, or a sale. It sounds good on its face, but what enriches the broker in the near term arguably costs that same broker longer term due to reduced volume. In other words, if trading is expensive, there will be less trading.

As Smith and other economists have often repeated, as the price of trading a good goes down, the amount of trading in the good increases, and usually exponentially. In the late 1980s, when it was twelve cents to twenty-five cents a share to trade, whether it was a single share or one million shares of a stock, a big day on the New York Stock Exchange was a day where one hundred million shares traded. Now that the price to trade equities has come down by more than 90 percent, it is routine for the number of shares to be traded on a single day to be counted in the billions.

Commissions on equity sales and purchases are still shrinking now to where investor websites like Robinhood and E-Trade offer commission-free trading. We say this was and is for the betterment of Wall Street, and the finance industry more broadly. This discussion will continue in the next chapter.

For now, it's useful to return to the abnormally high commission structure for realtors. We believe it harms all concerned, *including realtors*.

What's fascinating about commissions on home sales is how little they've changed. According to a 2021 study conducted by Notre Dame Law professor Roger Alford and Northwestern University's Benjamin Harris for *Regulation* magazine, real estate broker commissions have remained virtually unchanged for decades.[58] The latter is fascinating simply because the surest truth about prices of goods and services in a dynamic economy is that when markets are relatively unfettered, prices are relentlessly *falling*.

To give readers a feel for what we mean, we'll start with air conditioning. In a throwback to chapter 1, call air conditioning the "private jet" of the 1930s. You laugh? Once again, not so fast.

It wasn't until 1932 that the first window unit AC came on the market. The problem was that exceedingly few could afford such a luxury. In his 2016 book *America the Ingenious*, author Kevin Baker reported that the initial window-ledge models retailed in the *$10,000–$50,000* range.[59] To say that the air conditioners were well out of the price range for 99.9 percent of Americans in 1932 would bring new meaning to understatement. In Jack's Austin, Texas, The Tavern, a bar/restaurant that is surely an Austin "institution," has a flashing sign out front indicating the establishment is "Air Conditioned." This was once a big deal. Air conditioners were *sui generis*, which of course speaks to the genius of the profit motive. Nowadays, a cursory look on Amazon reveals all manner of window AC units that can be had for under $200. More on this in a bit too.

For now, it's worth considering other "standard" appliances of modern times that not too long ago were not. 2017 marked the fiftieth anniversary of the microwave oven. Back in 1967, Tappan microwaves could be had for $1,295, while nowadays exponentially more powerful and advanced ovens can be purchased on Amazon for well under $100.[60]

What about something as basic as the calculator? These are standard today on the supercomputers that we fit into our pockets and that are otherwise known as smartphones. In 1970, Texas Instruments released its first pocket calculator for the rather princely sum of *$400*.[61]

In a free-market economy it's the norm for luxuries to soon enough become everyday items. When markets are at work, what's scarce soon enough becomes abundant. Entrepreneurs attain great wealth by quite literally mass-producing what used to be nosebleed expensive.

Yet the commission cost of selling a home has barely budged for decades? In fact, according to Professor Maisy Wong from Penn, the fees paid to realtors have exceeded the inflation rate every year over the last seventy-five years, except for one. Notable here is that they've exceeded the inflation rate even though the cost of accessing information has plummeted. The previous truth is on its own quite something to contemplate. Indeed, in 1866, technology visionary Cyrus Field completed a transatlantic cable from the U.S. to England that enabled much quicker communication between the old and new world. Still, the transmission of information was incredibly costly. Back then, if you wanted to get quick word to London it would cost you ten dollars per word with a ten-word minimum![62] Nowadays, a simple internet connection on your pocket computer enables you to beam endless words and video around the world for next to nothing.

All of this is important in consideration of how the information revolution has transformed the process of finding and buying a house. While it could once again be argued that realtors earned their high commissions precisely because they were constantly pounding the proverbial pavement in pursuit of buyers and sellers of homes at best connected by classified ads, the internet has put voluminous information about houses, their interiors, their prices, monthly mortgage costs, mortgage lender options, and all sorts of other once difficult-to-attain information right at our fingertips. If you have an internet connection and/or a smartphone or computer, you can quite literally pinpoint the neighborhoods you're interested in, at which point you have access to enormously more housing information than realtors provided in the days before broadly accessible internet. As Jack's REX colleague Michael Toth explained it in a 2021 opinion piece for the *Wall Street Journal*, by the year

2020 "97% of buyers started their home search online, and without the assistance of an agent."[63]

Despite these basic truths, despite the very real truth that the house hunters and sellers of today are doing much more of the work previously done by realtors, commissions haven't moved. In other words, there's no real market at present for housing. It's very controlled.

Beyond all that, it's worth it to add that realtors are hardly scarce. More realistically there are a lot of them aggressively competing for your business. According to Roger Alford and Benjamin Harris, as of 2020 there were over one million realtors and over ninety thousand brokerages competing for the business of homeowners and homebuyers alike.[64] Despite this, despite feverish competition, the commissions related to selling yet again haven't moved much. By design. The NAR is powerful given its representation of 1.5 million members more than eager to maintain the commission status quo. The NAR maintains its power by requiring NAR membership so that brokers can attain access to multiple listing services (MLS) where houses are listed for sale. Access to the MLS is crucial when it comes to doing one's realtor job, but it also requires adherence to rules governing commissions paid to home sellers and buyers.

The MLS requires that the seller of a home executing a home sale must not only pay the fee to his own agent, but that they must also pay a large fee for a buyer's broker whether the buyer needs a broker or not. Yet most of the discovery of homes occurs online without an agent's assistance. Moreover, the seller must pay and provide for *all* the services for a full-service buyer agent whether the future buyer needs all of those services or not. In a real market, the buyer would buy those services for which he or she needs assistance, not purchase the others, and negotiate the price that he or she is willing to pay for those services that he or she does need, just as one does with every other service provider. But what is possible in every other industry is not possible in the NAR-controlled world of residential real estate agents.

The import of the buyer broker commission rule cannot be minimized. As Alford and Harris reveal, seller brokers must maintain the buying broker's commission in order to secure their access to the MLS, after which they note that "the MLS will not publish listings that do not include buyer broker commissions, and in all but one local market it *prohibits* buyers from knowing the compensation offered to their agents."[65]

Some will reply that for sale by owner (FSBO) sellers could list their houses on MLS, but in certain states there are regulations against doing just that. There's also a tendency among brokers to skip over the houses that are FSBO to discourage others from going that route.

Still others will reply that so much house hunting today involves driving neighborhood after neighborhood in search of the ideal house such that FSBOs are going to get as much attention as houses repped by brokers. It's a reasonable point too, though John can recall his parents selling their first house in Pasadena back in the late 1970s in FSBO style, only to find that realtors routinely stole the signs indicating the house for sale. His parents ultimately gave in to all sorts of pressure only to list with a realtor.

Whatever the ultimate answer, we're certainly aware of the happy truth long ago uttered by Jeff Bezos that "your margin is my opportunity." What's outsized and outrageous in terms of size, and housing commissions are just that, is ripe for the taking in the marketplace. Jack knows this well from his previous career at Goldman Sachs, plus he's living this truth now as he builds REX. Jack's intent is to break the stranglehold that NAR has long had on commissions.

Still, as evidenced by the non-movement of commission prices over decades, markets aren't fully at work in the housing sector. If they were, logic dictates that commissions would have come down long ago. Yet they're stuck.

That they are means that the cost of moving is enormous. Put another way, the very country made economically brilliant by the "restless" movement of human capital to its highest use is losing some of the movement informing that natural restlessness.

According to Alford and Harris, American mobility is down by one-third since the 1980s. This cannot be minimized simply because it's so counter to the American experience. Consider the latter relative to Italy. Referencing Moretti's *The New Geography of Jobs* once again, he noted that in his native country "most people spend their entire lives in the city where they were born." Conversely, in the U.S. "about half of American households change addresses every five years," which is a number "that would be unthinkable in Europe."[66]

The contrasts help explain all the frenzied economic activity in the U.S. versus the "Eurosclerosis" insults routinely thrown at the European economy by Americans. More than people want to say, *We're not European*, despite so many Americans being able to claim European ancestry. We're not Chinese, Mexican, Indian, or Nigerian either. We descend from the individuals who uniquely had get-up-and-go within them, who were willing to cross oceans and borders in pursuit of something better. Yes, we come by our mobility naturally. How sad then, that one of our greatest traits that renders us so different from others is neutered by taxes of a kind levied on movement in the form of the 5 to 6 percent brokerage fee.

There are many other ways the NAR/MLS use their rules to stop competition, and they'll be discussed in greater detail in this book's afteword. For now, when a trade group sets the terms of competition among its members, as Adam Smith wrote three hundred years ago, you can be sure that the consumer is being ripped off at sale, but also being shortchanged given the high cost of mobility.

In closing this chapter, an economy can't reach its full potential if immobilizing forces limit the movement of human capital to its best and most productive use. The costs associated with house sales ahead of moving are enormous, and rather unique to the United States where the NAR has proven more than effective at keeping in place a commission structure that brings new meaning to the concept of *immobilier* that we introduced in the previous chapter.

Jack's REX once again aims to break this commission stranglehold on sales and progress, but the NAR is a powerful entity. In other words, his success and that of others is by no means a given. In a U.S. economy that's long been defined by falling prices for everything, housing commissions remain immobile themselves. The irony here to us is that their immobility works to the detriment of realtors. Yes, you read that right. In the next chapter we'll discuss just that.

# CHAPTER FIVE

# What Boosts Human Capital Mobility Will Also Lift Realtors and the Economy at Large

*"The proportion between the real recompence of labour in different countries, it must be remembered, is naturally regulated, not by their actual wealth or poverty, but by their advancing, stationary, or declining condition."*

– Adam Smith, *The Wealth of Nations*, p. 218

"My clients will never check in at a front desk, they will never fill out any forms, they will never have a moment when their trip isn't absolutely seamless." Those are the words of Stacy Fischer-Rosenthal, president of Fischer Travel, and daughter of its founder, Bill Fischer. Their eponymous travel consultancy is generally viewed as the most expensive and exclusive of its kind in the world.

Eager to get a taste of Fischer Travel's services? Get in line. And curb your enthusiasm about gold-plated trips ahead. Odds are you'll never be *chosen* as a client of Fischer, and please don't think about calling to change Fischer-Rosenthal's mind. The number is unlisted.

On the other hand, if you're a big enough deal to rate being tapped as a Fischer client, get ready to pay through the nose before you board your first private jet. As *Robb Report's* Jackie Caradonio reported in 2019, the initiation fee alone to become a Fischer customer is $100,000. Tacked on to the latter is a $25,000 annual renewal fee, not to mention costs associated with the booking of each trip. And once again, you must be *chosen* as a client, or member, before achieving the privilege of paying exorbitant sums for the best in global travel. Caradonio reports Fischer has only 175 members.[67]

To be clear, Fischer is at the top of the travel consulting pyramid. There's no debating this truth. But in a book imbued with the view that progress is a consequence of human capital migrating to its highest use, along with the belief that the subsidies and taxes (commissions) on movement limit the migration, the evolution of travel consulting rates discussion.

It does, because back in the 1970s, travel agents were compensated very handsomely for doing very basic work. Airline tickets back in the "Me Decade" were extraordinarily pricey given high barriers to entry in the highly regulated airline space. Easily forgotten nowadays is that airlines were largely a creation of a federal government intent on moving mail around the U.S. more quickly. That airlines had a government origin meant that their routes were actually planned by the Civil Aeronautics Board in Washington, DC.[68] Yes, you read that right. Up until the late 1970s, federal officials in Washington planned airline routes as opposed to market forces. Don't worry, the story gets weirder!

As the end of the 1970s neared, the desire for airline deregulation grew. Republicans and conservatives loathe regulation, and they were intent on freeing up airlines to compete. Here's how one senator made his case for unshackling the airlines: "The problems of our economy have occurred, not as an outgrowth of laissez-faire, unbridled competition. They have occurred under the guidance of federal agencies, and under the umbrella of federal regulations." Good, free market stuff. Except that it wasn't a conservative Republican who made the previous statement; rather, it was none other than Senator Edward M. Kennedy in a debate with Eastern Airlines president Frank Borman on March 1, 1978. Borman sought to maintain "the orderly regulated marketplace."[69]

Needless to say, the U.S. Senate's "liberal lion" in Kennedy won thanks to articulate support of free markets and deregulation, only for the heavily regulated version of the airlines to thankfully reach its endpoint. On October 24, 1978, a Democrat president by the name of Jimmy Carter signed the Airline Deregulation Act into law.

The digression matters simply because reduced regulatory oversight in Washington set the stage for more entrants into the airline space, more realistic routes, and more competition for the traveler dollar on those routes. Airline fares declined in concert with the airlines ending their courtship of travel agents who'd historically been the order-takers for airlines, and who were paid a 10 percent commission on routinely expensive fares. At one time United Airlines' "Fly the friendly skies" advertisements had an addendum, "Call your travel agent." But as they say, all good things must come to an end, assuming agent reliance on ticket sales was a good thing. The main thing is that fares began to decline in the '80s to reflect competition, and then as most readers are likely aware, the internet began to reveal itself as a force in travel by the 1990s.

To offer up one of many examples, online travel site Expedia floated its shares to the public in 1999. John witnessed this up close at Goldman Sachs, and even allocated the company's IPO shares to his private clients. Expedia signaled a major change in how we would plan travel. Rather than asking a travel agent to compare fares, and rather than calling airlines, would-be travelers could fare shop on their own. And it didn't stop there as most readers know. Airlines weren't going to sit tight only to pay smaller commissions to Expedia and other competitors. They launched their own websites, and well into the 2000s would reward customers with mileage bonuses if they booked tickets on their sites online in lieu of calling airline representatives.

About the rapid change that industries enjoying big margins must eventually come to terms with, some in the world of travel weren't ready for it. Having come up as order-takers, what used to pay the bills in lucrative fashion no longer did. This is the stuff of dynamic growth: services we've grown used to and that providers have grown used to providing, are quickly replaced. When was your last "Blockbuster Night?"

With the internet having replaced all manner of travel agencies, no doubt it was assumed that travel agenting was over with. Such a view likely informs the aggressive way in which the NAR protects extraordinarily dated commission structures related to housing. Desperate to avoid the fate of many travel agencies made obsolete by the internet, the NAR fights to maintain the status quo based on the presumption that erasure of the existing commission structure for home sales exists as an existential threat to the realtors it represents. Such a view is short-sighted, and arguably insulting to those it represents.

Really, such a view assumes realtors aren't worth their exorbitant pay such that relentless bullying and lobbying is required to maintain it. The thinking is wrongheaded.

To see why, consider travel yet again. On its face, the internet was a major destroyer of jobs in the travel space. But that's a narrow way of looking at what happened. While the internet surely did replace ticket and hotel sales as a source of revenue for agents, it opened up all manner of new revenue sources for those who desired to work in travel. Think about it.

That which frees up labor provides rocket-fuel to the economy. Put another way, an internet that destroyed order-taker jobs that were a sub-optimal use of precious human capital freed that human capital to more productively deploy its talents. Better yet, the internet made workers of all stripes quite a bit more productive. Productivity is just another word for economic growth, and the internet was and is productivity personified.

The rising prosperity that the internet fostered proved glorious for travel professionals. It was as though the talented individuals in the travel space suddenly had ten to twenty assistants helping them help their customers. No longer required to spend endless, soul-crushing time booking airline tickets, those passionate about travel could suddenly pursue fee-based work whereby they would design trips for customers with means, and who wanted something unique.

While Fischer is once again at the top of the travel advisory pyramid, the list of fee-based travel-advisory services grows by the day. Freed from the rote work of booking tickets, these travel advisors increasingly take on the role of *portfolio managers* with a focus on travel. Instead of calling American Airlines to find the best route to Honolulu, travel professionals nowadays design multi-year travel plans for couples and families. Consider a family of four in which the kids are ages three and five. Travel planning in the here-and-now is going to be very different relative to the needs of parents and kids ten years from now. The travel advisor of today is not only tasked with designing memorable and rare excursions that won't be found on Expedia, that same travel advisor is tasked with creating "travel syllabi" that will evolve to reflect the age of those traveling. A trip to Orlando for spring break that makes perfect sense for families with kids five and eight, will not make sense for that same family with kids aged thirteen and sixteen.

Prosperous travelers also want exclusivity. They want what others haven't done, and the internet has arguably made what's *sui generis* much more of a possibility. Intrepid travel advisors may have had air-travel commissions taken from them by the

BRINGING ADAM SMITH INTO THE AMERICAN HOME

internet, but what technology takes, it gives back in much greater amount. The travel professional of today is much more of a well-compensated *sleuth* in search of what's rare.

The simple truth is that automation is the friend of the professional precisely because it's the equivalent of giving the professional "extra hands" to do great work with. With tickets automated, the professionals at Fischer can do the seemingly impossible. This ultra-exclusive agency is staffed with people who "ring" the concierge bell in the office when they move the proverbial mountain for members in ways that include securing a tennis lesson conducted by tennis legend John McEnroe, a private tour of the pyramids in Egypt,[70] or convincing the world's greatest hotels to literally knock down walls to create the setting required by members.[71] Fischer is yet again one of many travel firms recreating what it is to be a travel consultant in the age of rapid-fire communications that free individuals to routinely exceed their service potential.

And then there are travel influencers. While travel agents used to treasure being feted by airlines offering thanks for volume of tickets sold, the internet has spawned all manner of professional travelers who are quite literally paid to travel the world, all the while posting videos and weblogs about their excursions. So yes, the internet rendered ticket agents yesterday's news only to create much better work opportunities for individuals with intense passion for travel. We think the NAR, or better yet NAR members, should view the positive evolution of travel advisory as a model for what will happen if and when MLSs are opened up in markets nationwide in concert with aggressive liberalization of commissions. What appears terrifying and industry-crushing on its face won't destroy realtor jobs as much as it will propel realtors to a much higher level of professionalism, service, and pay. Adam Smith would agree. Work that is stationary in nature will inevitably be work defined by reduced compensation. The NAR has been successful so far in keeping commissions sticky, but what no longer makes sense won't last forever.

It was once asserted by Goldman Sachs partner Roy Zuckerberg to John's 1998 new associate class that "you don't sell 500,000 shares on E-Trade." Zuckerberg's point was that internet trading at low costs wouldn't put Goldman's legendary trading desk out of business as much as the automation of smaller transactions would free GS traders to more and more specialize in moving large blocks of stock. You wouldn't sell 500,000 shares on E-Trade simply because the sale of hundreds of thousands of shares would require a trader who knows the market for the company's shares well, and who knows how to sell them without moving the market in a way that would potentially bring on a loss for the seller.

Some will reply that 500,000 shares is no longer a large block, which is precisely the point. That which automates activity at much lower costs generally leads to a lot more of the activity. While it used to be that the commission on a sale of 500,000 shares would be enormous, automation has pushed down the commission "tax" on trading so that there's much more of it. 500,000 shares is no longer a big trade. Call it progress. No doubt the small trades aren't sent Goldman's way anymore, but hardly to the firm's detriment. Liquid markets defined by voluminous trading redound to the Goldmans of the world expert at buying and selling enormous share blocks in quiet fashion.

Which gets us to the realtor angle. The NAR is focused on maintaining 3 percent commissions each for the buying and selling broker, but arguably to the detriment of brokers. All this focus on protecting commissions regardless of home cost means that more than optimal time is spent by brokers in pursuit of the proverbial airline ticket order. Surely an abundance of these small sales adds up in commissions, but at what long-term cost? Just as happened with travel, transportation, and stock brokerage, when fees go down, the revenue loss is oftentimes more than offset by the huge increases in volume that occur with lower fees.

Spending precious time in pursuit of the 3 percent of $500,000 simply because that's the accepted commission rate means that brokers have less bandwidth to provide the bespoke services that have transformed travel consulting. If travel agents were still selling airline tickets they would be stuck in a stationary state decried by Smith in hot pursuit of 10 percent of a number that is in persistent decline thanks to competition.

Looked at through a housing prism, 3 percent for each side on home sale of $250,000–$500,000 amounts to a big chunk of the annual income for those who own such houses. And since the cost of buying and selling is so high, there's logically less of it. High commissions that amount to half of median American income render the market less liquid that it otherwise would be. Moving is expensive.

Conversely, imagine if the typical $250,000–$500,000 house were sold in a more E-Trade fashion on the internet, or for much smaller commissions related to less involved service from buying and selling brokers. No doubt this would reduce broker compensation per house sold, but there would logically be more houses being sold as always-restless Americans moved from house to house and city to city in hot pursuit of better opportunity and better housing with all the benefits to the American economy above. One can easily imagine a permanent increase in economic growth every year as it becomes nearly free to move about the country. We will discuss these huge knock-on effects to the U.S. economy in more detail in the following chapter.

More important, the automation of relatively low-cost housing sales would yet again free up the property passionate to spend their time providing tailored services a la Goldman Sachs to equity owners, and Fischer Travel to those eager to see lands near and far in all new ways. Put simply, high commissions are restraining their alleged beneficiaries.

About the above assertion, we should be clear that that the high commissions that are viewed as a "courteous" way of doing business aren't restraining *all* brokers. From television shows like Bravo's *Million Dollar Listing,* many readers are certainly aware that more than a few realtors are in the process of redefining how the business is conducted. Much like their counterparts in travel, they've used video to create "porn" for those who can't get enough of property. It's a reminder that markets move where they're supposed to move regardless of efforts by certain entities to maintain a stationary state.

As a result, the top realtors are much more than housing brokers of times past. Nowadays they consult with their clients on how to stage the house they have for sale for open houses, how to reach a broader audience through video, and how to find buyers.

Take a "realtor" corporation like The Agency that is featured prominently on *Million Dollar Listing Los Angeles*. The individuals in The Agency's employ are so much more than brokers. They're instead property experts helping their clients build real estate portfolios, financing them, all the while bringing to sellers a global network of buyers created by a team of professionals hailing from all points around the world. The days of open houses are likely numbered as well-connected property savants expertly connect the buyers and sellers from all over.

The internet yet again makes this possible. That which replaced the traditional stock and ticket broker, and that will logically replace the traditional broker of houses, is transforming the property business for the much, much better. Many readers doubtless remember this well by how panic over the coronavirus proved unequal to a never-ending American obsession with property—one that the virus arguably magnified as evidenced by at least a near-term rush out of cities. Open houses and private showings an impossibility? No problem. The internet enabled many more showings.

What's amazing about the online showings is that they were not just the creations of realtors. Just as the internet has spawned the well-heeled influencers of travel, so has this ever-improving technological advance created an opportunity for property influencers. Where it gets more interesting is that some aren't even realtors.

Enes Yilmazer is 31, and yes, has no broker's license. Despite this, a *Wall Street Journal* feature on the popular YouTube property personality indicated that he earns $50,000–$100,000 per month from YouTube ads run on his channel alone. Why can Yilmazer charge so much? He can because he's got somewhere north of 820,000 subscribers to his channel which features houses that bring new meaning to the previously mentioned "porn" that is real estate. If there's a remarkable house or apartment in Beverly Hills, California, or in the billionaire sections of Manhattan, or somewhere in between, Yilmazer is touring it with camera crew in tow. It seems the interest among YouTube viewers in $50–$100 million properties is endless.

Whereas he used to have to convince realtors to let him into the palaces they were looking to sell, his growing reach means they come to him. Yilmazer doesn't charge realtors for featuring the palatial properties, and he doesn't with good reason. It's those virtual tours that push all manner of subscribers his way. On the other hand, he's able to charge five figure fees to realtors who are marketing more middle-of-the-pack properties, not to mention the fees he gets for featuring different corporate brands in his videos.[72] Once again, what technology takes it gives back in spades. Its existence mocks traditional forms of compensation, but its reach is opening all manner of new ways to be compensated in the housing space. The limiting factor nowadays seems to be inventory.

Indeed, as the opening chapter made plain, there's limited housing available as this book is being written. To the latter, some readers are surely thinking Jack and John aren't seeing straight. Don't they remember 2008? Aren't they sentient to what's happening in 2023? Don't they know by now that all manias pass, and that they can pass in gruesome fashion, leaving those in "long" real estate to sell into a market bereft of buyers?

Yes, we do. Don't forget from chapter 1 our argument that housing consumption is a consequence of economic growth as opposed to a driver of it. Housing manias that render supply the bare-shelved equivalent of toilet paper in the spring of 2020 often die hard. Again, the music always stops. Consumption is what we do when we're not saving, and mass consumption signals a slowdown in the capital formation necessary for abundant growth. So yes, we again get it.

At the same time, housing's an American obsession. That's not going to change. Nor will it change that Americans are restless. Yet at present, there's a huge tax levied on the buying and selling of houses that is suffocating our restless ways. We say there's an answer to this problem of low housing supply combined with restlessness. The NAR must get out of the way.

The entity charged with protecting the interests of realtors must protect them by ending what will ultimately be a losing battle anyway. The only question is whether realtors and the NAR win by "losing" now and "winning in the near future" versus "winning" now only to lose in the not-terribly-distant future.

Why are we so confident the NAR will ultimately lose? We are because the internet's production of voluminous information is soon enough going to turn every potential homebuyer into an information machine that will render the typical, commission-seeking realtor yesterday's news. Think about it.

As we've already reported, 97 percent of home searches begin online as is. For the typical home purchase, we no longer need many aspects of the brokers.

Better yet, it will increasingly be possible for prospective buyers to act as realtors do now: studying neighborhoods, sales in neighborhoods, modeling comp sales in neighborhoods on the way to making informed offers. No doubt the NAR and realtors hanging on for dear life will keep houses off of MLSs, but watch as buyers and sellers more and more work around listing services only to literally knock on doors of owned houses with offer in hand, only to make a purchase without either side swallowing commission costs.

If readers doubt what's ahead, they need only drive any neighborhood. In doing this, they need only look up any house to find on their smartphone abundant information about the house's selling history, what it last sold for, time on market when it was sold, what its estimated value is, and so on. Anyone with a car and a smartphone, or better yet, feet with a smart-phone, can very quickly attain detailed acquisition knowledge of a neighborhood that almost certainly exceeds the knowledge brought by realtors before the Age of the Internet began. The simple truth is that we don't need realtors nearly as much as we used to thanks to technological advance.

Will the internet kill off the realtor? A resounding no! What it will do is force a rationalization of commissions that, much like what Jack experienced at Goldman Sachs, will greatly increase the frequency of home sales. With a major tax effectively removed from the home-selling process by *progress*, there will be quite a bit more home-buying and -selling. What realtors will lose in commission percentages will be more than made back through volume of selling. Watch as realtors in pursuit of commissions now evolve as fee-based consultants as they help the property-focused build portfolios.

Arguably most important, with the largest cost of home-selling greatly reduced, the economy will get a boost for two obvious reasons. For one, falling prices as this book has hopefully made plain signal economic progress. What saves us money certainly fosters new demands, but the better, more economy-enhancing truth is that what saves us money enhances our ability to save and invest. For two, what frees us to migrate our talents to their highest use is what frees us as individuals to prosper the most. It's what frees us to specialize, and when we're specialized our income logically increases to the betterment of the housing market overall.

Rest assured, that the benefits to realtors, influencers, and others associated with housing will paradoxically increase as commissions are either allowed to shrink, or are forced to shrink by progress. A booming economy is ultimately the best friend of sectors reliant on consumption, and any progress made in reducing the tax on movement would surely redound to the economy.

Will the internet ultimately cut out the realtor middle man altogether on houses in the $250,000–$500,000 range? The speculation here is yes, but we also speculate that few will care in much the same way that few travel professionals lament any longer the disappearance of the 10 percent commission on airline ticket sales. It's the past.

What's important to remember is what's been regularly stated in this chapter: technology always gives back much more than it takes. While technology will increase all manner of realtor-free transactions among buyers and sellers aggressively using the internet, to paraphrase Jack's Goldman partner Roy Zuckerberg, exceedingly few will go to Zillow, Redfin, or Realtor.com to list their $4 million mansion or $10 million estate.

In short, realtors will lose some, but not all of the smaller transactions, but the alleged "loss" will be made up for by myriad other high-end gains. The simple truth is that exceedingly few owners of high-end property are going to handle these sales on their own. Instead, they'll go to increasingly specialized brokers a la The Agency and yes, REX, in search of wildly personalized service as they sell and buy. And to increase buzz, they'll go to the many Enes Yilmazers of the world in pursuit of the viral buzz that only the internet can provide.

In closing, the future is beautiful for realtors...if they'll let it be. What will be beautiful for increasingly well-compensated realtors will also redound to the typical homeowner, and for reasons beyond an end to nosebleed commissions that restrict mobility, or that make mobility an incredibly costly notion.

CHAPTER SIX

# High Housing Sales Commissions Restrict Investment, and by Extension, Job Creation

> *"Whatever obstructs the free circulation*
> *of labour from one employment to*
> *another, obstructs that of stock likewise;*
> *the quantity of stock which can be*
> *employed in any branch of business*
> *depending very much upon that of the*
> *labour which can be employed in it."*
>
> – Adam Smith, *The Wealth of Nations*, p. 156

"Romans will eat pizza, here and there, they will eat it anywhere." Those were the words of *New York Times* reporter Elisabetta Povoledo, in a June 2021 dispatch from Rome. They love their pizza in Italy, though one always wonders what they think of our

Americanized versions that we consume with abandon. But that's a digression.

Given the worship of pizza where it originated, it's only natural that entrepreneurs would consistently look for new ways to meet the needs of ravenous consumers. What's adored is lucrative for the providers of that which is adored.

Which brings us to Massimo Bucolo. A former medical device salesman, Bucolo has created pizza vending machines that make it from scratch in three minutes. What a story on its own! Entrepreneurs are always searching for ways to make our lives easier, and in Bucolo's case pizza in three minutes out of a standalone machine might simplify things for us. In his own words, "I'm not trying to compete with pizzerias, I'm proposing an alternative."

While pizza has for the longest time been the ultimate delivered food, the wait is usually thirty minutes or more. Bucolo is looking to shrink the wait. Unsurprisingly, he has doubters.

Even though Bucolo is clear that he's not trying to compete with sit-down pizzerias, owners of same are skeptical. Povoledo quotes Renzo Panattoni, owner of "the Morgue," which is one of Rome's most prominent pizza restaurants, as being "dismissive" about Bucolo's vision. In his words, vending-machine pizza "has nothing to do with traditional pizza."[73]

The definition of an entrepreneur is generally someone who believes deeply in something, or a way of providing a service, that is roundly rejected by most everyone else. Think about it. Entrepreneurs are by their very descriptor trying to change ingrained habits, but habits die hard. Better yet, if a new way of commerce were obvious, or were viewed positively in the world of commerce, the good or service would already exist. Again, entrepreneurs are generally in pursuit of what's ridiculed. They quite literally aim to change how we work, play, shop, and eat (among other things), and they're trying in the face of immense skepticism.

This hopefully explains why Silicon Valley is littered with venture capitalists who passed on Facebook, Google, and Amazon. What's obvious in retrospect is rarely that way in real time. Long-time fans of Amazon know this truth well. For the longest time, Jeff Bezos's now multi-trillion-dollar creation was billed "Amazon.org." Get it?

This new concept most certainly made it possible for us to buy books, CDs, and DVDs with ease, but it couldn't make money. It could only lose money. The odd presumption occasionally revealed itself in Amazon's stock price, among many other sources of skepticism. In other words, for much of its existence Amazon's shares at times wilted in the face of existential threats, real and perceived. In its first twenty years as a public company, Amazon's shares corrected at least 20 percent at least one time for sixteen of those twenty years.[74] Put in much crueler terms, the world is littered with investors who sold Amazon shares for very little that, if they'd just held on to them, would be worth millions, tens of millions, and *billions* today. Readers might keep all of this in mind when thinking about Amazon founder Jeff Bezos, and why someone worth over $200 billion hasn't paid more than the billions he's already paid in taxes. He hasn't because Bezos held on to Amazon shares that all too many investors lost faith in over the years.

The great entrepreneurs generally see a future that's unimaginable, which is why they're so rich.

Bucolo and Bezos are worthwhile anecdotes to begin this chapter for what visionary entrepreneurialism says more broadly about opportunity for the rest of us. While Bucolo is "dismissed" now by the competition, the future of commerce is opaque. Bezos was endlessly dismissed. Just as Bucolo likely isn't being inundated now with resumes, readers can rest assured that Bezos wasn't being showered with CVs in 2001 (when Amazon's shares collapsed into the single digits) in the way that the company he formerly ran is in 2024. There's an important story about human migration within entrepreneurial achievement. Amazon helps tell it.

As is well known, Amazon is based in Seattle, WA. Its immense success since opening its doors in Bellevue in 1994 has proven a magnet for the Pacific Northwest among strivers from around the U.S., and around the world. By its twentieth year as a public company in 2017, Amazon had shed its ".org" tag. It was the bluest of blue chips. Workforce is an essential driver of the latter. Amazon's had grown fast. As of 2017, it employed three hundred thousand people around the world. It reached that number faster than any company ever had before it.[75]

By 2021, Amazon had reached seventy-five thousand employees in Seattle alone. Yes, it's proven a major lure for the Emerald City. So much so that in concert with its growth, Amazon has pursued ways to increase affordable housing.[76] Who would have guessed it? Really, it cannot be stressed enough how unlikely housing shortages in Seattle once were.

You see, little more than forty years ago Seattle was, in the words of Enrico Moretti, "closer to today's Detroit than to Silicon Valley." *The Economist* magazine had labeled it the "city of despair," while describing it as a "vast pawn shop, with families selling everything they can do without to get money to buy food and pay the rent." As opposed to Seattle having an affordable housing problem, no such dilemma existed then. Quite famously a billboard was put up near the airport that said, "Will the last person leaving SEATTLE – Turn out the lights."[77] Seattle was a city in freefall. Consequently, housing was cheap to reflect the mass exodus of its best and brightest, along with surely some dimmer bulbs too.

Oh well, how things change. In 1979, what was then Micro-Soft moved from Albuquerque to Bellevue. Luckily for Seattle, Bill Gates and Paul Allen were natives of the "city of despair." They saw beauty where others didn't. Much like Amazon's arrival in the 1990s, no one could have possibly taken Micro-Soft's relocation seriously. In the 1970s it was still assumed personal computers would never be a thing. They were way too expensive. As Digital Equipment CEO Ken Olsen put it in the 1970s: "There is no reason for any individual to have a computer in their home."[78] Software for personal computers? Come on! Shopping on the internet? Come on!

Readers know the story. Microsoft went on to become the world's most valuable company, and its founder in Gates the world's richest man. Success attracts talent, and talent flowed to a city that was once most notable for repelling the homegrown and skilled. Twenty-five years later Amazon opened its doors, as previously mentioned in Bellevue, WA. Thanks to Microsoft's stratospheric success, by the 1990s Seattle was thick with the engineering and computer talent Bezos would need to staff his nascent corporation bent on changing how we shop. And the rest is history.

The Detroit of the 1970s and '80s is now a booming city in 2023. Seattle can claim two of the world's five most valuable companies, and many more name brands like Costco, Nordstrom, and Starbucks. Call it a rich city. *Big time.*

This is important from a human migration perspective simply because successful entrepreneurial endeavor tends to have a multiplicative aspect when it comes to jobs. Applied to Seattle, and quoting Moretti yet again, "high tech jobs are the *cause* of local prosperity," and then all the jobs that emerge from high-tech plenty "are the *effect.*" Some will doubtless reply that most lack the skills to be high-tech workers, thus rendering all this talk about the location of high tech a moot point for the common man. The reply would be mistaken. Indeed, Moretti's research on Apple alone found that of the tens of thousands of non-Apple jobs that were a consequence of Apple being in Cupertino, many more were unskilled than skilled.[79]

What's true in Cupertino, CA is also true in Seattle. The high average compensation at Microsoft that is of the six-figure variety for the company's employees leads to all manner of service jobs—from investment banking, legal, and money management on the high level, to baristas, restaurant servers, and security guards on the lower end.

The crucial economic truth to consider when thinking about entrepreneurial genius is that it's very hard to pinpoint where it will be. Again, Microsoft moved to Seattle in 1979.

Rest assured that the *Wall Street Journal* and *Forbes* didn't high-light the move in their pages. Amazon's arrival in 1994 similarly wasn't notable to the chroniclers of commercial advance. Stating what should be obvious, if reporters had had a clue about the significance of Microsoft and Amazon when they got to Bellevue, they quite simply wouldn't be reporters. They would instead presently be centi-millionaires and billionaires. It's that simple. And it's no different in Cupertino, CA. When Steve Jobs returned in 1997, Apple was headed for bankruptcy, only to be saved by none other than Bill Gates. Put more clearly, investors didn't think Jobs could right Apple's faltering ship.[80] Again, how things change.

And since things change so quickly, so, too, does the location of jobs and job opportunity. Commercial genius surely results in immense job creation well beyond the successful company itself, and the job creation is broad—from highly skilled to more manual work. What's crucial is that individuals be mobile in pursuit of the opportunity that will reveal itself, often in unexpected fashion. In a legal and transportation sense, they already are. As we discussed in the earlier chapters, the U.S. is the ultimate zone of commerce. We can go any-where, and we have countless choices in terms of how to go anywhere. People aren't so lucky in the Congo. As stated early on, one of the biggest drivers of American prosperity is our freedom to move to where opportunity is greatest. Except that some of us are stuck.

About this, trust us that we're not making victim arguments here. If you're born in the United States, you're born on second base as it were, but often on third. Americans have it so good relative to the rest of the world.

Still, as we've made plain, the cost of selling one's house is quite a bit more expensive in the United States. The commissions we pay on home sales amount to a big tax that makes it more costly than it otherwise would be to be mobile. For perhaps more typical Americans, moving has become incredibly costly as evidenced by commissions on home sales amounting to a quarter, and often half of the median American income. The increasingly stuck nature of American life certainly has an economic impact.

To see why, let's look back to the Adam Smith quote that begins this chapter: *"Whatever obstructs the free circulation of labour from one employment to another, obstructs that of stock likewise."* Smith's point was that investment follows talent. That it does is kind of obvious, but perhaps something that's easily forgotten.

In Smith's words yet again, the "most decisive mark of the prosperity of any country is the increase of the number of inhabitants." So true. Think Bezos again, but think also the talented people Amazon hires. Think the same for Mark Zuckerberg and others. There's a constant battle for talent among businesses, and the migration of that talent dictates corporate success. In the words of Zuckerberg, "Someone who is exceptional in their role is not just a little bit better than someone who is pretty good. They are 100 times better."[81] In other words, the best recruiters of talent will oversee the most successful companies.

American housing commissions are an excessive price placed on mobility, but they're also a price suffered by corporations for the prices slowing the flow of labor. Some will say this is now mitigated by Zoom and other advances that reached fame during the coronavirus lockdowns, but that seems a stretch. We know this because people working together, and bouncing ideas off of each other, are able to innovate more and faster. It is extremely hard to recreate the serendipity of a good idea, or the realization of a hidden problem through the small talk that occurs spontaneously in a shared physical space. Moreover, there is the hard truth in building a new business that "culture eats strategy for breakfast." It is exceedingly difficult to build up a unique and strong culture on Zoom. A strong culture requires personal interaction. Moreover, culture is passed horizontally from employee to employee, vertically from the founder to the new recruit through the modeling of personal actions, and through the mimicking of behaviors, which of course and by definition only happens in person.

Steve Jobs designed Apple's Cupertino campus with random meetups among employees top of mind. So while commissions amount to an expensive burden on the well-to-do always in search of better opportunity, it's most of all a burden on the more typical American.

Most Americans know this, at least obliquely, from their experiences in 2020. Amid the lockdowns related to the coronavirus, crowded city living was rendered less attractive relative to suburban homesteading. As a consequence, a "migration mania" soon revealed itself.

As Ali Wolf, chief economist for housing market research firm Zonda explained it in a July 2021 opinion piece for the *New York Times*, remote work during the lockdowns had "untethered" many American workers from their "physical offices."[82] Of course, there was a monetary aspect to the untethering. Per Wolf, those with "higher-income jobs" were most likely able to work from home. Not so, for lower-income people. As one study about the layoffs during the lockdowns revealed in gut-wrenching fashion, nearly 40 percent of households earning less than $40,000 a year suffered at least one job loss in March of 2020, 19 percent of households earning between $40,000 and $100,000 experienced a layoff, and then 13 percent for households earning over $100,000.[83] Those with the least suffered the lockdowns the most in a job-loss sense.

They also did in a housing sense. Indeed, and as has been documented throughout this book, demand for housing in 2020–2021 far exceeded supply. This challenged those with the least in a price sense, but also in a selling-and-moving sense. For obvious reasons.

While swallowing 5 to 6 percent in home-sale commissions perhaps didn't mean too much to "buyers whose wealth allowed them to win bidding wars often with a high down payment and a bid over asking price,"[84] this would mean a lot to the more conventional buyer. Again, a home sale of $500,000 is going to generate commissions that are likely half of the income for all too many Americans. That they're so high logically limited supply for prospective homeowners who lacked abundant wealth, but it also limited the willingness of more conventional homeowners to put their houses on the market. Selling a house is expensive. Very much so.

As it stands now, high commissions on housing don't just set back the realty industry; they hold many homeowners in a stationary state, rendering them sitting ducks in a rapidly morphing economy. Those same high commissions are a real problem for those with the least. That they are not only limits supply of houses, but it also limits the ability of the financially constrained to migrate their talents to their best use. If mobility is going to be very costly, everyone loses.

Per the Smith quote that begins this chapter, this constrained mobility of labor will have a definite economic impact precisely because it will alter the flow of the very investment that drives all economic growth. Capital flows quite simply follow human flows, the flow of humans is the signal of where prosperity will be and where it will no longer be, and right now artificially high commissions born of lobbying heft, laws, and theoretically tradition are holding back greater movement that, if greater, would result in even more substantive prosperity.

Never forget that the most important driver of housing health is prosperity itself. Housing vitality is yet again a consequence of prosperity that is a consequence of capital migrating to its highest use. Entrepreneurs are mobile, but not necessarily the hundreds of thousands (and millions—Amazon presently employs 1.2 million) who would more readily move to where entrepreneurial endeavor is transforming life as we know it. High housing commissions plainly factor in limits on mobility that fall on the middle the most. Let's liberalize them. No one will lose.

# CHAPTER SEVEN

# My Talent, and My Choice of What to Do with It

*"It frequently happens that while high wages are given to the workmen in one manufacture, those in another are obliged to content themselves with bare subsistence. The one is in an advancing state, and has, therefore, a continual demand for new hands: The other is in a declining state, and the super-abundance of hands is continually increasing."*

– Adam Smith, *The Wealth of Nations*, p. 155

"Get back on the goddamned plane at five o'clock and go back down to school. If you don't, you ain't got a family." So said Dominic Marocco to his younger brother, Frank. It was the 1950s, and young

Frank's football prowess had won him a football scholarship at North Carolina State.

Cliched as it may sound to some readers, football was Marocco's ticket out of Aliquippa, PA. If he chose to, Marocco would get to pursue work far from Aliquippa's various factories and mills operated by J&L Steel, the city of Aliquippa's primary employer. That's what his brothers wanted.

So eager was Dominic to get Frank out of Aliquippa, he actually got him a job at a J&L tin mill before college so that he could see through the sweat and sand why he wanted to attain education and a college degree that would free him from J&L's rather dirty work. Marocco wasn't alone. "Big Mike" Ditka, father of NFL great Mike, worked in Aliquippa's mills, but "didn't want his four kids working the mill, too." For son Mike, a "high school tour of J&L killed any interest in a job there." Wes Dorsett, father of NFL Hall of Famer Tony Dorsett, warned his kids, "Come in this place, you don't know if you're coming out. And if you do you might be missing an arm or eye or leg. Do *something* for yourself."

Hopefully readers get the picture. Mobility doesn't just have economic qualities; it also has life and death qualities. But the main genius of mobility is it frees us to pursue what elevates us. By the second half of the twentieth century, an Aliquippa, PA that had once been a magnet for strivers from around the world because it "had the work," was repelling its best and brightest. Parents, brothers, and sisters were doing the pushing. As S. L. Price explained it in his spectacular 2017 history of Aliquippa, titled *Playing Through the Whistle*, "Nobody grew up with the dream to work" the factories of Aliquippa. "They were filthy, boring, exhausting grinds, a drain on health, a daily assault on the senses."

Marocco's brothers were doing this "filthy, boring, exhausting" work for a living. They wanted better for their younger brother. They wanted him back on that "goddamned" plane so that he could avoid their fate. The story about Marocco and his caring brothers is a cautionary tale for those easily taken in politicians promising to bring back the past. No doubt many readers are more than familiar with ambitious politicians who promise to "bring back" the factory jobs that moved "overseas." When they make such nonsensical pronouncements, they're loudly advertising their ignorance. Those who knew Aliquippa's factories and mills knew well how dreary and life threatening the toil was. They wanted nothing to do with it. Worse, a promise to bring back the past is a not-so-veiled promise to take the economy backwards. Adam Smith was clear that even a stationary employment state repels the very investment that boosts wages and the quality of our work, so imagine the investment associated with economic activity moving backwards. Put another way, when politicians pledge to bring back the past, they're promising intense misery born of lower wages and collapsing living standards.

The better, pro-growth political approach is for politicians to pledge that they will roll out the welcome mat for the commercially talented. It's remarkably skillful individuals who attract the investment that results in broad economic opportunity. If anyone doubts this, imagine if Jeff Bezos announced a plan to move himself and his family to Aliquippa with a plan to start an all-new business. The investment that would follow

Bezos on the way to soaring job creation in the once prosperous town would be staggering. *People* drive progress, not empty pledges about the past.

Of course, it's often the case that politicians don't grasp the above truth. Stagnation is the result. Hard as it is to imagine now, there was a time when Flint, Michigan, could claim the highest average income and the lowest unemployment rate in the U.S.[85] This was true back when the automobile industry was Silicon Valley in stature such that the best and brightest were flocking to Michigan, and investment was following them. It's a reminder that closed factories didn't shrink the economic behemoth that Michigan once was, but the departure of talented people surely *did* seal the state's fate. The talented migrate away from the past, and instead pursue an advancing state of economic affairs a la Smith. It cannot be stressed enough that politicians promising the past, or clinging to the past, are doing major damage to those with the least by driving away the most economically capable. Marocco's story, and the story of mass migration out of Aliquippa more broadly is indicative of this truth. And it's a reminder yet again of how lucky Americans are to live in the U.S. Paraphrasing flight attendants, they're free to move about all fifty states without limit. *They can get out.* They can follow the talent if a declining or stationary state is repelling the talent.

This rates regular mention not just because mobility is so limited in places like the Congo, but also because it was so limited in places like England at one time. As the Smith quote that begins this chapter alludes, where you are can determine how much you can earn if your mobility is limited. The wages in locales where industry is evolving are very different from where industry is stationary in nature. This matters simply because mobility in Smith's day wasn't a given.

Smith noted that the people of England were exposed to just this "oppression without remedy." Their movement wasn't free. England's Poor Laws ensured just that. With an eye on limiting the number of workers in certain towns, England's misguided leaders aimed to keep the price of labor artificially high. They misunderstood work in the way that all too many politicians misunderstand it now.

Higher wages aren't a consequence of worker scarcity. If they were, the highest paid workers would be in largely depopulated locales like Flint, Detroit, and yes, Aliquippa. What moves worker pay upward is the productivity of the work, not a numerical lack of workers. In much the same way, an increase in the number of "hands" doesn't shrink worker pay. The level of investment in workers is what defines their pay, which explains why compensation in heavily populated cities is most often greater than pay in lightly populated locales. Smith vivifies this truth well:

"It is by means of an additional capital only that the undertaker of any work can provide his workmen with better machinery, or make a more proper distribution of employment among them."

For the longest time able-bodied people have been coming to the U.S. from around the world, and investment has followed their migration. Once in the U.S., they've similarly been free to move about. This freedom of movement was logically a lure for people who wanted something better. And again, it wasn't always this way in Smith's England. There were laws limiting movement on the assumption that too many workers would drive down wages. Such a view was very backwards, and Smith knew this well. Worse, it was cruel to use geography to limit one's opportunities, yet that was what prevailed in eighteenth century England. In Smith's words, "To remove a man who has committed no misdemeanors from the parish where he chuses to reside, is an evident violation of natural liberty and justice."

Fast forward to the present, and in the United States there are no real legal limits to human migration. At the same time, there are artificial ones. From the previous chapters readers are very aware of artificially high commissions that have a regressive quality to them, and that make moving very expensive.

There are also taxes themselves, or proposed taxes. For background, the federal tax code includes Section 1031, which is a one-hundred-year-old provision. And while we reject the popular view that real estate is "investment" in the traditional, Adam Smith sense, it cannot once again be denied that housing is an essential good that many with means invest in with an eye on turning investment profits. Section 1031 exists as a tax incentive for property investors to do just that: develop property and housing in hopes of turning a profit.

Getting into specifics, Section 1031 "provides real estate investors a tax deferral on the financial gain of a [property] sale if they roll the proceeds directly into a similar investment property within 180 days."[86] To the latter, some will say tax favoritism is at work, and they won't get much pushback from us. In an ideal world the fruits of savings and investment wouldn't be taxed at all. There are quite simply no companies and no jobs without investment first, and just the same, there's logically less housing stock if there are tax penalties levied on the building or rehabbing of same. The taxing of work and the savings that make work possible bring new meaning to perverse. But we digress. Back to Section 1031.

The Biden administration has put a bull's-eye on the section. As Joe Gose of the *New York Times* explained it, President Biden would like to rein in this aspect of the tax code since Section 1031 is said to "benefit the wealthy and not workers."[87] The view is shortsighted, and worse, just plain incorrect.

Indeed, it cannot be forgotten that the movement of houses to one set of hands to other sets results in all manner of valuable work for those facilitating the transactions. Gose himself mentions services related to insurance, title, and inspection, among others. Better yet, the transactional only tells part of the story.

The bigger story is the *why* behind the purchase or "investment" in the real-estate property in the first place. Individuals are buying the house or houses with a goal of selling same at a profit. Their vision of profit more often than not is rooted in a plan to improve the house on the way to setting it up to fetch more dollars in the open market. In other words, the property investments made by individuals yearning for profit from resale may enrich the skilled real estate speculators among us, but generally only insofar as their focus on home and apartment improvement lines the pockets of those not rich. In this case, think the handymen, plumbers, painters, construction workers, electricians, HVAC installers, and countless other "working class" types who are employed by profit-motivated investment in housing stock.

It's a basic truism that with every transfer of a house from one owner to another, there's all manner of enhancing taking place after the transfer is completed, and sometimes before. It's a reminder that sticky commission structures don't just paradoxically hold down realtors freed from necessary evolution that would improve their work and compensation. These attempts to freeze the present in place limit liquidity in the property market that also greatly limits opportunity for the typical worker. The general rule is that on the margin, if you tax something, you get less of it. Artificially high commissions logically limit liquidity in the housing sector, and a proposed tax increase on investors pursuing home improvement would similarly have a chilling effect.

The above would harm the typical worker in a number of ways. For one, a highly liquid housing market is one that once again produces abundant work for plumbers, electricians, construction workers, and so on. How odd that self-styled "middle-class" Joe would seek tax changes so inimical to the Scranton, PA–types he claims kinship with.

For two, enhanced, more liquid housing stock would create greater ease for poor and middle-class owners to sell, but also presumably expand the range of options when they're *buying*. This is important. Movement within the zone of prosperity that is the United States is a big driver of individual prosperity. We need more of it, so artificial and tax code barriers to the buying and selling of housing are harmful to those with the least.

Which brings us back to the Smith quote that begins this chapter. He was writing of the segregation of able-bodied by parish via the country's Poor Laws, and how the limits on their mobility consigned the unlucky to very backwards forms of labor. In modern times, it would be the equivalent of forcing those born and raised in Aliquippa to stay there, and at the same time removing from more prosperous Philadelphia and Pittsburgh any "Quips" who had the temerity to migrate their talents to better, more investment-laden opportunities.

Thankfully Americans are yet again free to move as they wish in ways that eighteenth century Brits were not allowed to. Still, readers might think a bit more deeply about the modern, twenty-first century applications of Smith's thinking in the eighteenth.

While wise minds can (and surely do) disagree about the import of education to career success (John thinks the correlation weak), there's the reasonably expressed view that one's educational attainment can be limited by one's zip code. If you lack the funds in the U.S. to attend private schools, your school choice will largely be limited to where you live. That's all well and good if you're in Highland Park (TX), San Marino (CA), or Winnetka (IL), but not so if you're in—you guessed it—Aliquippa. At Aliquippa High School, a study on student academic achievement from the late 1980s found that 60 percent of the students were reading below grade level, 62 percent performing below grade level in math, and in a broad sense, the students within the Aliquippa school systems routinely finished close to the bottom in state rankings for math, science, reading, and writing.[88]

All of this speaks to the importance of mobility for reasons beyond jobs. Sometimes it's just as important *for kids* that parents be as free as possible to move without the various commissions, taxes, and barriers to mobility needlessly erected. Really, even if you're skeptical about education's import, few are skeptical about the importance of safety while at school. All of this speaks to the simple truth that barriers to mobility aren't just economically unfortunate, but also potentially unfortunate in the educational and safety sense.

Some chant that your zip code shouldn't decide your future. The chant seems overdone in a sense, but not totally unreasonable. There are barriers to mobility that are holding Americans back. Some of them are related to housing and ownership. Let's remove them, while also maintaining our skepticism about housing as an investment on its own. Which is where the next chapter will take us.

CHAPTER EIGHT

# A Case Against Home Ownership

*"Men are much more likely to discover
easier and readier methods of attaining
any object, when the sole attention of
their minds is directed toward that
single object, than when it is dissipated
among a great variety of things."*
– Adam Smith, *The Wealth of Nations*, p. 9

"**N**obody has ever done anything like this before
– not even the legendary Babe." Those are the
words of Jared Diamond, a *Wall Street Journal*
reporter whose beat is oddly enough professional sports.

Diamond's subject? Los Angeles Angels star pitcher *and*
hitter Shohei Ohtani. As for the "Babe," Diamond meant the
legendary Babe Ruth; Ruth is easily on any Mt. Rushmore of
Major League Baseball (MLB) greats for his home run hitting
prowess. Ruth retired from the game in 1935 with 714 home

runs. His record stood for nearly forty years, until April 8, 1974, when Hank Aaron hit his 715th.

What's interesting about Ruth, but that some readers may not know, is that he entered professional baseball as a pitcher. A very good pitcher at that. In 1916 and 1917, he won forty-seven games in concert with an earned run average of 1.88.

Yet as good as Ruth was as a hurler, it soon became apparent that he was an even better hitter. Diamond reports that on May 6, 1918, Ruth started at first base for the Boston Red Sox, only to hit a home run. He homered the next day too, and really never looked back. Diamond notes that his "pitching appearances became more sporadic" as the excitement about his batting skills became more and more pronounced. Better yet, a bio of Ruth indicates that he "often feigned exhaustion or a sore arm to avoid the mound." According to Diamond, Ruth started nineteen games as a pitcher during the 1918 season, fifteen during the 1919 season, after which he was acquired by the New York Yankees only for the "two-way experiment" to essentially end. Ruth pitched just five games for the rest of his career.[89]

Ruth's exit from pitching surely changed things. After 1918, baseball, like realistically all forms of work, became more specialized. For the better. While it was long known that Ruth was exceedingly rare in his ability to hit and pitch, it wasn't until the 1970s that the American League finally acknowledged what was long known: pitchers are rarely good hitters. We're talking about two different skills. And so the designated hitter (DH) was born in Major League Baseball's American League. The National League has held out on the matter, or remained "pure," at which point baseball minds can debate the good or bad for the game of pitchers hitting. The main thing is that pitchers who are good hitters are rare.

Which is why Shohei Ohtani is such a phenomenon. As of mid-season in 2021, Ohtani wasn't just the Angels' best pitcher. His statistics at the plate put him at the top of the AL in terms of home runs, slugging percentage, not to mention that he could lay claim to twelve stolen bases at a time when stolen bases are increasingly rare. Ohtani was selected for the MLB All-Star Game as a hitter *and* a pitcher. That's what Diamond meant about Ohtani's on-field exploits exceeding those of "even the legendary Babe." In 2021, at a time when the game of baseball is more specialized than ever, Ohtani is hitting and pitching at elite levels. If the Babe were alive, it's reasonable to believe that even he would be impressed. Diamond cites a 1918 interview Ruth conducted with *Baseball Magazine* in which he observed, "I don't think a man can pitch in his regular turn, and play every other game at some other position, and keep that pace year after year."[90] Yet that's what Ohtani is doing, and rates immense admiration inside and outside the sports world. Those watching Ohtani have never seen anything like his achievements. Which is the point.

Rare is the individual who can specialize in a variety of pursuits at the highest of levels. Ohtani is a major story precisely because what he's doing is so rare. *There's no one like him*, and arguably there never was.

Back among us mere mortals, if we're lucky, smart, or both, we pursue the kind of work most commensurate with our skills. The more specialized we are in what we do, the more productive we are. If readers doubt this, they need only imagine doing their present work in addition to raising and growing the food they eat, sewing their clothes, and constructing their shelter. The realistic answer is that if we had to fend for ourselves in addition to doing our day jobs, we would be exceedingly poor. *Desperately poor* while also flailing at our specialty. In John's case, he doesn't hide from the basic truth if he had to produce his own food, clothing, and shelter that he would quickly die a writer who hadn't written anything, while wholly bereft of food, clothing, and shelter.

Going back to chapters 2 and 3 in particular, specialization on the job is our best friend. By far. When we can focus on what we do best, it's no longer work in a sense. Our productivity as specialized individuals soars given the basic truth that it's fun to do what we're really good at. Shohei Ohtani is a joy to behold, but to paraphrase warnings from television ads: "*Don't try this at home.*" Luckily most of us don't have to. Thanks to increasingly unfettered trade with producers around the world, we can more and more focus our minds "toward that single object," only to exchange the fruits of our labor for all that we want and need.

Stated simply, trade elevates us precisely because it frees us from doing what we're no good at doing. In a scholastic sense, free trade is the equivalent of a lover of all literature (who despises math) being told that school will be reading and writing all day and every day, with no calculus exams to worry about. Amen to that!

We know from Adam Smith that an advancing state of work elevates the individual, and that narrowly focused workers are much more productive precisely because they've in many instances happened on just the kind of toil that fits their skill set. All of this explains why robots will, contrary to conventional wisdom, be the best friend of eager workers. What automates human action also frees humans to specialize even more. The future of work is beautiful, and of a kind where exponentially more of us will be the Michael Jordan of our profession. Bank on it.

Which brings us back to home ownership. We think that for many it's a big, expensive, and needless barrier to brilliance on the job, and wealth accumulation. We say this even though Jack is building a business around helping people achieve home ownership with better service and better results, but at lower commission costs. Don't worry about the industry; Jack certainly isn't. Housing's still an American obsession, and it will remain one despite our case against home ownership. REX will be just fine.

Still, it's worth thinking a bit more deeply about what we're taking on when we purchase a home. And to focus on the costs associated with it, including sick-inducing monthly mortgage payments, is to mostly miss the point.

We say "mostly" because monthly mortgage payments, or even all-cash housing purchases, rate consideration in terms of what you're giving up. You're realistically giving up a lot of future wealth in your pursuit of the home ownership that some consider the American dream. Indeed, while housing has morphed into more of an investment in modern times, a look back to chapter 1 will remind readers that over time the stock market well outpaces housing. Looked at through an all-cash or mortgage-funded purchase of a home, if the goal is long-term returns, you're most likely giving up much better returns over time. By tying so much of your wealth and/or income in housing, you're missing out on much better returns that can be had over time in the stock market.

To which some will understandably point to chapter 2 of *Bringing Adam Smith into the American Home* with an eye on the 1970s and 2000s. In both instances, housing was tops as an "asset class," and surely outperformed stocks. Some might similarly point to 2020–2022 in order to make their case.

It's all fair enough, but the fact remains that housing well underperforms the stock market over the *long term*, and that's the case we're making. Over the long run, savings directed toward the stock market will enrich individuals far more than those directed to housing. Importantly, this shouldn't surprise anyone.

Going back to chapter 1 yet again, a purchase of a house isn't going to open foreign markets, or cure cancer, or lead to remarkable technological advance. A house just *is*, while a profit-focused business attracts investment precisely because those running the business are relentlessly pushing themselves and their employees to achieve more and more. A house in many ways is as we see it, plus gradual enhancements, while the shape and breadth of a successful business just grows and grows.

Also, businesses in a dynamic economy fail a great deal as this book has made plain. There's no certainty in them, while with housing there's a lot more certainty. As we discussed in chapter 2, the rush into housing in the 2000s was in many ways a rush away from risk, while aggressive investment in businesses and entrepreneurial concepts is the process whereby we greatly dial up the risk we're associating our savings with. Traditional investing is quite simply riskier than traditional home "investment," and because it is, it's no surprise that the returns on traditional investing of the stock-market variety leads to higher returns. It does because the risk is greater.

That's why we stress long term once again. While the ups and downs of equity investing will be much more pronounced than home-price movements over time, over the long term the returns are much greater. Think long term. Invest in the stock market and forget about it. Just as we don't (and realistically can't) look up the precise value of the house we're living in on a daily basis, we shouldn't (even though we can) look up the prices of our public equity investments each day. Better to sit back passively, in much the same way as we do with a house.

After that, it's useful to point out what's not discussed nearly enough: the stock market's outperformance of housing returns only tells part of a much bigger story. Remember how we said that a focus on mortgage payments as a reason to not own a home "mostly" misses the point? The previous assertion is crucial.

That's the case because the main reason to avoid home ownership has to do with the ownership of the house itself amounting to a big leap away from the core competencies of the typical individual. Really, what do you the homeowner (or prospective homeowner) know about fixing toilets, showers, and sinks, or painting interiors and exteriors, purchasing HVACs for central air conditioning, installing a new bathtub, or adding on a room? What do you realistically know about hiring individuals to do all those things? To say that Americans are flying blind when they take the housing ownership leap is one of those statements of the blindingly obvious. As Adam Smith would point out, just as he did with the barley, the bread, and the beer manufacturer, each party is better off doing what they do best and then trading.

Because Adam Smith has been figuratively "locked out" of the American home, each homeowner is the potential "mark" for vendors who know a lot. Homeowners comparatively know very little.

If there are doubters, consider a visit to the mechanic with your car. You say you "trust" your mechanic, and maybe he's truly a prince in the sense that you're never taken advantage of. But are you sure? How could you know? What about what the mechanic does under the hood do you truly understand, and how much do you understand when he tells you what he needs to do in order to fix your car? The speculation here is that most who claim an understanding are fibbing. A little some of the time, but most often a lot.

Some evidence supporting the above claim about mechanical illiteracy has to do with the offer of all manner of drivetrain warranties these days, along with offers to prospective buyers to purchase protection in advance against major visits to the mechanic. Since we don't know, we pay a lot up front to ensure that we're essentially insured against future problems with the car's engine. Translated, we don't truly know what mechanics are saying, so it's better to be insured through warranties.

Even better, it's safe to say that we more and more lease cars not just because the latter theoretically positions us to drive what we couldn't afford if we had to purchase it all at once. Another endorsement of car leases is that they free us from having to be mechanics, or from having to play one during visits to the mechanic. Leases essentially allow us to "outsource" our car problems to the actual owners of cars, and to whom we compensate for the car's depreciation while we drive it. Leases include maintenance, which is what we want.

Please think about this through the prism of home ownership. While a walk into a house isn't as incomprehensible as opening up the hood of an automobile, what's inside any house is machinery well beyond the ability of most any homeowner to grasp. If the plumber says you need a new garbage disposal, are you really positioned to question the assertion? What about a new air conditioner? As for that shower in the guest bedroom, does fixing the drip really require several hours of work, or is the fix actually one that can be measured in minutes?

The simple truth is that we don't know these answers. While we're often experts at work such that we can confidently discuss matters related to our specialty, how confident are we when we're discussing maintenance issues related to the powder room's lighting?

Readers know the answers to the questions, some are doubtless sheepish about them, but per Niall Ferguson in the introductory chapter, housing's an obsession among us. Basically we work tirelessly to achieve specialization on the job that affords us home ownership, at which point we spend the fruits of work in enormous amounts so that we can own that which is expensive, and that is incomprehensible to the vast majority of us.

It all begs us to consider the unseen. It's not just the mortgage or cash costs of owning a house, it's not just the maintenance costs that we most often accept somewhat blindly from people as confident about what they're doing as we are about our jobs, it's the costs associated with our spending precious time on what we don't understand. What do we lose on the job, on a job that fits our skills, by doing what has nothing to do with our skills? The answer is that home ownership likely doesn't just cost us in reduced investment returns, and in overpayment for housing fixes and improvements the cost of which we can't understand. It arguably costs us the most in unseen ways as we exit our specialty as a pitcher in order to hit the proverbial baseball.

What a mistake. Think again back to chapter 3. As discussed then, arguably the most famous passages from *The Wealth of Nations* were the early ones about the butcher and baker pursuing their narrow self-interest in meeting our needs. They were specializing, and they are. More important, consider the pin factory mentioned. Men working alone could maybe produce one pin per day, but working together with other men on narrow specialties, they could produce tens of thousands.

Please consider all of this with home ownership top of mind. Ownership is when we step out of what we understand, when we take calculus all day every day even though our expertise is literature.

To which some will ask something along the lines of what choice do we have? Housing is essential. Housing shelters us, plus it's a good hedge against currency devaluation. All of this in mind, homeownership's positives outweigh its demerits.

To all of the above, we say it's all true.

But in a book that aims to make readers think differently about housing, we ask readers to also consider a very different future when it comes to homeownership. Since most owners are not fit to do the endless work that comes with home ownership, our expectation is that markets will provide a solution. Our bet is that in the coming decades more and more businesses will open that offer to "partner" with prospective owners. Those eager for shelter, and yes, an inflation hedge, will partner with businesses that know how to manage an actual house. Through the partnership, the pressures of ownership will soon be lifted from owners. In other words, they'll get their focus back. "The sole attention of their minds" will be on their real jobs that enable ownership, and not on fixing or hiring the fixers of what they can't begin to understand. Basically, we foresee a future defined by co-buyers of houses: the principal owner and the actual house manager.

Still others will simply go the "warranty" route, albeit for homes. Since most of us don't have a clue, we'll have a would-be house manager inspect the house being purchased ahead of time, only for the inspector to come back with a quote on the cost of outsourcing home management.

Adam Smith was so wise, but arguably wisest on the matter of labor division. It's essential to progress, but has largely been pushed aside by an obsession. We propose to bring Smith back into the home in all ways, including how people own. And they'll grow wealthier in the bargain, which makes sense. Smith's ideas of freedom and free markets were philosophical, but they attracted global attention that lives to this day because

JOHN TAMNY & JACK RYAN

people understandably worship at the altar of wealth. What's crucial is that full home ownership doesn't foster the latter, which is why we make a case against home ownership, albeit a nuanced one.

# CONCLUSION

*"It is not the actual greatness of national wealth, but its continual increase, which occasions the rise in the wages of labour. It is not, accordingly, in the richest countries, but in the most thriving, or in those which are growing rich the fastest, that the wages of labour are highest."*

– Adam Smith, *The Wealth of Nations*, p. 79

"We need to get the economy back in a safe way," and "give people [the] confidence they're going to be able to participate in the economy." So said Florida governor Ron DeSantis on April 19, 2020.[91]

While the Sunshine State was the last of the major states to lock down in 2020 (April 1)[92], lock down it did. And the economy suffered mightily. Florida's economy is one very reliant on tourism, yet suddenly convention centers, hotels, theme parks and other tourist draws were shuttered. So were bars and night-clubs, while restaurant operations were reduced to takeout and delivery. The shutdowns coincided with 650,000 unemployment claims by Floridians in the first month alone.[93]

Is it any wonder that DeSantis was eager to reopen Florida's economy? As anyone who's ever lost a job knows well, it's agony. Most would say it's worse than sickness, and it's a trauma that can stay with us for many years. Florida would be one of the last states to lock down, but also one of the quickest to reopen. Out of economic necessity.

Think Disney alone. This one corporation has such a profound impact on Florida's economy. One out of fifty Floridians is either directly employed by Disney or has a job related to its immense economic footprint in the state. In central Florida, the economic heft of Disney is even greater.[94] A closed Disney World would logically ripple through the state's economy. Something had to be done, and it was.

It's also worth keeping in mind that Florida's schools were similarly in person and open by the fall of 2020. While school districts in California were still largely remote, DeSantis had an "all in, all the time" approach to schooling. Kids would be in classrooms.[95] The economic impact of this cannot be minimized. More than many may want to acknowledge, school has day-care qualities to it for parents. And if schools are closed, or virtual, the ability of parents to work becomes much more than a challenge.

DeSantis reopened Florida's economy early, but his relatively quick reopening of the schools similarly had economic overtones. They were also a signaling device to other Americans.

Florida was "open for business" as it were, its teachers were teaching, and both truths no doubt resonated with Americans at a time when so many city and state economies across the U.S. were still in lockdown mode to varying degrees, and when so many schools were still closed. By reopening the Florida economy and Florida schools, DeSantis laid out the welcome mat to all manner of non-Floridians.

One speculates that more than a few Californians viewed Florida in longing fashion. While DeSantis strove to make his state hospitable to business during a rather fraught period, Los Angeles mayor Eric Garcetti announced that water and power would be shut off to all "non-essential" businesses in the City of Angels.[96] While DeSantis recognized the importance of businesses getting back to normal, California governor Gavin Newsom was recommending that restaurant patrons put their masks back on between bites as though COVID-19 took a break while people were actively chewing.[97]

There was a very free aspect to Florida that wasn't wholly apparent in California. Same with Texas relative to California. The Lone Star State locked down one day before Florida, but two weeks after California. It also opened up more quickly. Amid this Elon Musk announced a move to Austin, Texas, along with Oracle.

And it wasn't just the shutdowns in 2020 that inspired movement. As most readers likely already know, Texas and Florida can claim zero tax rates, while states like California and New York have top income tax rates that can sometimes reach the teens. Throw in more accessible housing, and it's not surprising that well before the shutdowns, eight Californians were moving to Austin alone each day as previously mentioned in chapter 3.

Talented people drive economic growth, and in 2020, governors like DeSantis in Florida and Greg Abbott were making a case that talent would be more warmly received, while taxed and regulated less in Texas and Florida. Clearly some moved, some did not, but the question for the purposes of this book would be about the "unseen." How many avoided migration to theoretically better living conditions because the cost of doing so was so great?

Such a question is particularly relevant to California when the cost of housing there is taken into account. High housing prices produce higher commissions. The "unseen" question to ask is how many more Californians would have exited a state defined by certain challenges if the market for housing had liquid, frictionless qualities in the way that the stock market increasingly does. About this question, it's one that has good meaning for California, along with the states that it's losing population to. Put another way, it does California no good if artificial barriers make departure from the Golden State too costly. For one, as we know from the examples provided about Germany and France from chapter 4, what's expensive to terminate is expensive to engage with in the first place. In other words, if exiting California becomes too costly, the state will lose for some not entering it in the first place. But there's more. Again, it's not healthy when artificial barriers restrain the termination or exit.

The above assertion may surprise some, but market signals are precious for all concerned. If California's tax, regulatory, and lockdown policies are really making Californians unhappy, a near-frictionless ability of Californians to exit the state would benefit the Golden State for it providing a clear message to the state's top policymakers. What suffocates market signals blinds us, and this includes policymakers. In other words, artificial commission structures that make moving more difficult do the locale being moved from no favors. For California to change, it must experience a sufficient loss of talent so that not changing is no longer an option. Of course, some would reasonably say the state doesn't need to change…

What's that, you say? Yes, some Californians say the state is doing just fine, that while it routinely loses middle earners eager to purchase more house outside the state, it routinely attracts the world's best and brightest. There's some truth to this assertion. Lots of it.

To understand the above better, it's useful to look at facts over media-driven narratives. While a *Wall Street Journal* editorial asserts that the departure of businesses from California to low-tax states like Florida "has exploded" due to high taxes and onerous regulations, it's worth pointing out that this editorial was penned back in 2011.[98] Basically, pundits have been writing California's obituary for decades, only for the state to continue to prosper.

While talk is endless of a mass departure of the world's most valuable companies (Apple, Amazon, Facebook, Google, and Microsoft), three of them are based in California. And it's not likely to change if market signals are to be believed.

To see why, consider venture capital investment in the decade since the aforementioned *Journal* editorial indicated a mass exodus of business. Investors with actual money on the line saw something entirely different. Indeed, while venture capital investment into Texas has doubled from $1.5 billion to $3 billion since 2011, it's more than *quadrupled* from $13 billion to $60 billion in California.[99]

So, what makes the Golden State so attractive to the talented beyond natural beauty, top universities, and yes, inertia? How do they overcome high taxation and regulation, along with occasionally authoritarian leadership? A possible answer to the California riddle is one that plainly has Adam Smith-style overtones. Expensive as California may be, overtaxed as it may be, people are very free to move around California, from company to company, sans friction.

As a 2016 piece in *TechCrunch* observed,

> ...one of the least celebrated and most fundamental drivers of [California's] success is an obscure-but-powerful legal provision passed into law back in 1872. In that year, the California Civil Code was amended to include the following language: "Except as provided in this chapter, every contract by which anyone is restrained from engaging in a lawful profession, trade, or business of any kind is to that extent void."[100]

The passage from *TechCrunch* has Smith-ian overtones. Think about it. California can't limit the movement of talent to its highest use.

Consider another piece of commentary from *Vox* in 2017.

The fact that any employee can quit and start his or her own rival firm is a key reason for Silicon Valley's success over the last half century. And it's made possible by an unusual characteristic of California law: Courts there refuse to enforce contracts that limit employee |mobility.

This rule has helped to cement Silicon Valley's role as the nation's capital for high-tech innovation. It ensures that powerful incumbents can never keep good ideas bottled up inside their walls. Ideas naturally flow to whichever company can best put them to use.[101]

It's probably fairly simple at this point for readers to connect the dots. In a book whose major theme is to make frictionless the movement of people to their highest economic pursuit, the why behind California's continued economic prominence isn't too hard to fathom. The simple truth is that a Google employee with an innovative idea can put out his own start-up shingle with great rapidity, and without fear of lawsuits for taking his talents elsewhere.

No doubt California has economic demerits that are too numerous to list here, but talent is the ultimate driver of economic progress. Of course, sometimes for talent to realize its potential, it must migrate. Authoritarian as California can be in some ways, it's laissez faire in others. Some of California's policy negatives repel population, but it just the same cannot be forgotten that investment follows commercial ability, talent, innovative minds, clusters of the skilled, the sophisticated; pick your adjective. Whatever it is, investment flows indicate that the economically capable continue to flock to the west coast.

About where people are going, and why they're going, this book isn't meant to explain the *why*. Instead, *Bringing Adam Smith into the American Home* is meant to get people to think about housing differently, how to perhaps own it differently, and most of all, how to remove housing as a barrier to the mobility that has long authored so much prosperity in the U.S. and still does.

We accept the obsession with housing and ownership, we accept that nothing much will alter the obsession (including differences in investment returns), but we don't accept the artificial barriers erected to movement in and out of houses, and in and out of cities and states that needlessly limit the human mobility so essential to progress.

Our goal with this purposely slim book was to showcase some of the artificial barriers (including home ownership itself) as a way of helping readers to think more expansively about what they're doing when they join the "landed," but also to get those who help them join the "landed" (think realtors) to contemplate what they're doing with the long term more in mind. In particular, we want realtors to recognize that the stationary state of their profession, one made stationary by a powerful realtor lobby in the NAR, is doing its presumed beneficiaries no favors.

No doubt the opposite may seem true in the near term, but market forces will inevitably weigh in. In other words, change is coming to the realty profession, whether the NAR likes it or not. Margins, real or artificial, ensure just such change. We say it's better for realtors to be out front of the inevitable change (as some already are), rather than be victims of same.

The main thing is that the change made inevitable by the democratization of information signals a better future in terms of mobility, but also a hopefully more liquid housing market that makes ownership less of a ball and chain keeping individuals from realizing their potential. After which, it's our hope that we changed minds about the nature of home ownership itself. There are so many reasons to own a home, but exceedingly few to manage what we own.

What's made all of this project fun is that the great Adam Smith's teachings from centuries ago have proven yet again how relevant they are to the present, and surely well beyond. Our book is a reminder that Smith's wisdom is timeless, and that homeowners and renters alike would be much better off if we brought Smith into the American home.

Jack Ryan
Austin, TX
John Tamny
Bethesda, MD
August 14, 2023

# Adam Smith Can Only Work in Free Markets

*People of the same trade seldom meet*
*together, even for merriment and*
*diversion, but the conversation ends*
*in a conspiracy against the public, or*
*in some contrivance to raise prices.*

*The Wealth of Nations*, Book I, Chapter X

"There are probably twenty people looking at your company right now." I was twenty-eight years old. On the other end of the phone was the CEO of 3M. "Jake" Jacobson was willing to take my call for a simple reason—fear. Why would a CEO of a large corporation take a call from a third-year associate at Goldman Sachs? Because it was 1988. Corporate raiders like Robert Bass, Carl Icahn, Kirk Kerkorian, Victor Posner, Boone Pickens, and Ron Perelman were on the hunt. It was a unique time.

After business school and law school, but before I joined Goldman Sachs, I had moved to south Texas and worked in an immigrant refugee camp. I helped Central Americans who fled Communist aggression find a place to live and work in the U.S. Realizing what I was doing was not what we today would call "scalable," I left the refugee camp for Goldman, hoping I would learn how to build an organization. Having the ability to speak to CEOs of large companies at a young age would help me learn what to do to build a successful organization that could impact lots of others who needed a break, but which could also scale.

I started at Goldman Sachs in 1986. As a junior investment banker, my boss and the future secretary of the treasury, Hank Paulson, called me into his office. He gave me a list of fifty companies, very few if any were corporate clients of Goldman Sachs. My job was to make them so. In this period, raid preparedness or "anti-raid" as we called it, was the way to do so. Hence, my call to Jake Jacobson and about forty-nine other CEOs. Given that Goldman was known not to help raiders, I, surprising even to myself, could cold call CEOs of very large public companies and they would take my call. Even more surprising, I would soon have a meeting with this CEO of the Fortune 500 company despite being only three years out of graduate school. And the way in was to show the CEO what Adam Smith's invisible hand would do to quickly redirect him if the CEO did not move fast to understand what a third-party raider would do, and then preempt that raid by taking those actions before the raider did. So, in many ways while it would not be sensible today, it was indeed very rational for the CEO to take my call at this singular period in the U.S. economy.

In the 1980s, levering up to acquire almost any public company was a fairly easy game. Many industrial companies had gotten fat and slow. After World War II, many of the international competitors that may have driven U.S. companies to be lean and mean were out of business. Destroyed by the war, it would take a generation for these international companies to be competitive again. So, while the rest of the world was rebuilding, many companies had taken the artificial and transitory phenomenon after the war, with little tough competition to conclude that they themselves were responsible for the success of the company. Staffs became bloated, innovation was not crucial without competitive forces pushing them to dream beyond their current abilities, earnings growth rates were not exceptional or if they were, often it was because there was no serious competition from Asia or Europe. It was the Era of the Imperial CEO. Like stock pickers in a bull market or the fly on the back of Aesop's chariot amazed at how fast he could fly, the CEOs thought *they* were the reason for their success. A few times they were. More often they were not, the whip had been pulled from Adam Smith's invisible hand, and the absence of the lash made many CEOs think they were exceptional. Without lots of competitive companies, many firms had lost their intensity.

Not only did many public companies lose focus on their core competencies where they had a competitive advantage, but even worse, they also took their success in a world of limited competition to mean that they could be excellent at managing almost any business, even outside their core expertise. This hubris extended to many firms. Publicly traded companies like Beatrice Holdings were, for example, in the food business, the women's underwear business, the travel bag business, the bottled water and water purification business, the candy business, the hand dryer business, the outdoor grill business, the industrial chemical business, the leisure apparel business, the garden equipment business, the children's play products business, to name just some of their businesses. Moreover, there were many more companies just like Beatrice, where Smith's lessons of division of labor, assets managed by their highest and best user, and competitive advantage had been forgotten because Smith had lost the attention of pupils in the classroom. He was not able to show failing grades because there were fewer competitors to give CEOs a test.

In addition to the emergence of competition from Europe and the East in the 1980s, another form of market discipline was quickly emerging. With the rapid development of a market for non-investment-grade bonds, individuals who on their own did not have much capital could lever up and make cash offers to pay substantial premiums to public companies' stock prices. This financing ability meant that if the managers of public companies were not catalyzed into action by emerging competition from other countries, a second and even larger threat was emerging to their livelihoods and reputations. Individuals without great amounts of equity capital could raise the money to pay a substantial premium to the stockholders of a company, gain a majority stake in the company, throw the existing managers out, and then work to cut costs, streamline the company, and refocus the company on businesses where they had a sustainable competitive advantage.

The playbook was almost always the same for what the mainstream press called a "raider" and not particularly complicated: (1) acquire a 5 percent stake in the public company in the open market, silently acquiring the shares through purchases through an investment bank; (2) file the 13(d) mandated by the SEC when an individual's ownership stake crosses the 5 percent threshold; (3) that public filing would immediately put the company " in play," as the *Wall Street Journal* and others would report on their front pages that an "unfriendly" investor had taken a 5 percent stake in a public company. "In play" meant that because one person found an opportunity and put money behind it, every strategic acquiror or financial player would look to see if they could pay more than the current stock price for the company or act as a "white knight" for the target company.

The CEO of the company was thus now one of the weakest animals in the business jungle with many predators of all shapes and sizes circling the company to take out the CEO, analyzing to see if they could do better than the originator of the first wound. Moreover, large owners of the stock owed no personal loyalty to the incumbent CEO. These investors were willing to sell to the highest bidder for their stock. "White knights" of the circled company were available to "help," but only if the company were sold to them.

While these individuals who initially put the company in play were called "raiders" and their actions were called "unfriendly," in the end they were making companies much more efficient in their existing operations and forcing the specialization of labor that Adam Smith had long ago proved would result in assets moving to their highest and best use and therefore to the most efficient and productive owners of the assets. Their actions were certainly not unfriendly to the shareholders who got large premiums to the current stock price. They were only raiders from the perspective of the incumbent management team.

The ramifications for all public companies, even those that had not yet been raided, were enormous. After decades of complacency, suddenly the lash of Adam Smith's invisible hand was everywhere, aggressively snapped by both the non-investment-grade debt market that made nearly every financial player a potential acquiror, and the reemergence of international companies entering the U.S. with more efficient business systems. The management of every U.S. company felt they had to move fast to streamline and focus their business to fend off raiders and foreign competition, lest they lose their high-paying jobs and publicly embarrassed as someone else took the necessary managerial actions for them.

Because Goldman was one of the very few large banks that would not help the raiders with financing or advising on "hostile" acquisitions, CEOs of large companies were much more willing to take a call from Goldman Sachs and share internal information with them, rather than potentially engage in a conversation with a bank that could flip on them and in a few months be on the other end of an unfriendly offer for their company. Thus, they would take my call whereas the calls of my competitors were less likely to be answered.

My pitch was almost the same, true, and helpful to the CEO. My suggestion to the CEO was that they hire Goldman to come into the company, go through all the internal numbers for each of the company's businesses, subsidiaries, and divisions, line by line, down to the most minute of expenses. We would also undertake a valuation of every business in their portfolio to see if someone else would be willing to pay a lot more for that division using their managerial acumen rather than that business being run by the current management team and valued within their current corporate structure by the public markets.

In the end, we acted as the company's internal corporate raider with a whiskey eye for even the most trivial of corporate expenses. In many ways, we war-gamed how we could drive a 40 percent or larger appreciation in the stock if we were an unfriendly player who wanted to make a quick return on an investment in the company. We would share our findings with the CEO, suggesting that they consider getting in front of a possible raid by doing some of the things that a raider would do, none of which was rocket science. This is what we called the "self-help" option, which was the client rapidly taking the streamlining actions themselves to preempt the unfriendly offer. The intensity of management teams across all U.S. industries increased dramatically.

By following the self-help remedy, companies performed better operationally as they focused on the businesses where they had a competitive advantage and disposed of assets for which they were not the best managers. Then the company would use the increased cash generated by their operations and the cash generated through the sale of underutilized assets to buy back their own shares. Thus, their earnings per share would usually increase due to the increased earnings over fewer shares outstanding. Moreover, the earnings per share growth rate would also increase for the same reason, thereby driving a higher multiple on the increased earnings, The company's valuation was significantly increased.

The shareholders certainly didn't view offers of large premiums to their current stock price as unfriendly or hostile in any way at all. This view was only held by the management team. Nor did they view the lash of the whip from Adam Smith's invisible hand to streamline, focus, and speed the growth of the company's remaining businesses as anything other than the necessary discipline needed to make companies and management teams their best value and version of themselves.

Adam Smith, unshackled by the very free financial markets in the U.S., forced discipline and rationalization upon U.S. corporations that stood the economy in good shape for the next thirty years as public companies became streamlined, focused, and efficient. The entire U.S. economy was improved, which provided for higher wages, more jobs, lower inflation, and more wealth for American families.

So, in the 1980s and 1990s, the way to improve businesses and even whole industries was from the right-hand side of the balance sheet. The catalyzers of change would use debt and other financial instruments that lived on the right hand of the balance sheet to take over the company and with their new control rapidly drive productivity and efficiency. This threat was amplified by new competitors arising from overseas who could beat the U.S.-based businesses in the marketplace or who themselves would take over U.S. companies and apply their more intense and more modern management skills to the underperforming U.S. company.

It was a great learning environment. I was able to sit at the elbow of some of the best executives in the U.S. as they made their decisions in a very disruptive environment. I learned how to scale organizations, drive efficiencies, attract money, recruit excellent people, and build cultures that could create massive competitive advantages. One of the main reasons I had left the refugee camp, where I felt I was helping too few too slowly, had been fulfilled by the business world. I had learned how to grow organizations within the white-hot fire of competition.

What does this have to do with the U.S. housing industry? Today, in the early part of the twenty-first century, the exact same thing I described above is happening once again across all industries and the entire U.S. economy. However, with one big, stark, and reliable difference:

Today, the disruption is coming from the *left-hand side of the balance sheet*, not as an attack from the righthand side. However, the end result or "creative destruction" as the great economist Joseph Schumpeter called it, is just the same.

Today the way to attack inefficiencies, establish great cultures, improve the customer experience, create wealth, and generate superior shareholder returns is to harness the tools of the twenty-first century. These tools include: (a) the widespread and free flow of data through the internet which bridged many information moats formerly held by middlemen, (b) harnessing artificial intelligence tools to make business predictions from the massive amounts of information and data collected through the web, (c) creating technology stacks that can directly change the companies' tactics, the employees' actions, and customer interactions in response to changed markets or consumer demand in seconds or milliseconds, and (d) building a culture within the new companies of "fast, fast, fast" improvement through "test, learn, and iterate"—deploying improved customer experiences as predicted by data in the fastest way possible. This rapid deployment of new business practices within seconds or minutes requires a very different mindset among the humans engaged in the enterprise. The business is dependent upon immediate action. It is not the case that the incumbents are as fat today as they were in the 1980s and 1990s in the sense of bloated expense structures, unfocused businesses, and high-cost balance sheets. It is the case that many have outdated business practices given the rise of super-technologies which can only be remedied by recreating assets from the ground up.

Driven again by the power of Adam Smith's hand, the raiders of the *twenty-first* century are those who would rebuild the assets of a company or whole industries around a data collection and intelligence stack, recreating the asset side of the balance sheet. Using the right-hand balance sheet to take over companies to focus the enterprise, drive out expenses, and reduce the cost of financing had been done in the prior shareholder revolution. Today's shareholder revolution comes from the left-hand side.

Today's businesses utilizing new assets built from the ground up can provide much better service, create better customer outcomes, and do so at a fraction of the prices of the incumbents' cost structure. Witness what has happened to well-run but outdated travel agencies, taxi dispatchers, and yes, stockbrokers. They indeed had all been streamlined after the '80s and '90s. Yet, their way of doing business had become ossified again.

External threats had led to the first corporate revolution. External threats drive the second. The incumbent's technical debt is often overwhelming, and their employees are often not best of breed in artificial intelligence or big data. Furthermore, they did not have the ability to make super-fast changes to the benefit of the customer due to the extremely rapid consumption and processing of millions of pieces of data.

All of the broker industries mentioned above have been replaced by brand new companies such as Schwab, Uber, and Expedia with more efficient business models built around completely different asset and business models than the assets of the high-commission competitors they replaced in the form of E.F. Hutton, Yellow Cab Company, and Carlson Travel. In fact, it is so arduous a task to change their business models, their cultures, and their tech stacks that unless faced with a similar external threat as were the fat corporations of the '80s and '90s by the emergence of the raider and international competition, it was unlikely to be done this time around either.

Furthermore, John and I learned from our experiences at Goldman that company culture is the most important asset, and also the most difficult of assets to transform. Cultures at the incumbents that could not be changed to succeed in a fast, fast, fast world with technology driving human performance, known as "AI with humans in the loop" inevitably fall victim to the speed and intensity of a tech-centered collection of individuals in the same industry, where data is much more important than the hierarchies of seniority or experience. Cultural transformations can usually only be completely rehabilitated by a dire threat from the outside.

Therefore, just as in the 1980s and 1900s, Adam Smith has been unleashed in the twenty-first century again with lash in hand again to force businesses into much more efficient forms of themselves. And just like in the 1980s and 1990s, every industry in the U.S. is currently being changed by these intense outside competitive forces to run their businesses in much different ways—or have been made obsolete by these new tech-enabled forces. Especially every industry that had acted as a middleman for consumers has been replaced. The internet is the new middleman, with better service, outcomes, and prices 70 to 90 percent lower on average.

That is, every industry except for one.

The one industry that has not been made more efficient through the creation of different ways of doing business, as this book has shown, is the residential real estate industry. Of tremendous importance, this industry is one of the largest in the U.S. with approximately $50 trillion of underlying assets. Moreover, the industry is many times larger than this amount from the point of view of the business service provider because of all the services attached to the home, such as mortgages, title insurance, escrow services, home insurance, and managing the home. These other services entail about $40 trillion in mortgages, $50 trillion of home insurance, $50 trillion of title insurance, escrow services for $50 trillion in assets, and the $1–$2 trillion of outsourced home maintenance each year.

Yet despite the extreme profit potential given both the size of the fees for the above services and their tens of millions of transactions per year, something had blocked Adam Smith, again, from reforming the largest industry in the U.S. in the way that every other industry had been reformed. Not only had he been blocked from improving this industry once, but now he had been blocked twice. How was it that this industry alone had survived the two prior revolutions and still employed assets, business structures, people skills, and cultures that had become obsolete thirty-five years ago? There is no natural explanation other than a massive wall created by the industry that blocked Adam Smith and thus the consumer from enjoying the benefits that went to the end customer in every other industry. Breaking the blockade is why Lynley Sides and I founded REX. We wanted to bring the shareholder revolution and consumer-first orientation to the largest industry in the U.S., which had successfully and supernaturally kept competition out for decades. The middleman, in the form of the expensive and highly commissioned agent, diminished in power in every other industry by the web, was still the most important player in this industry.

In housing, the customer is both the homeowner and a shareholder. It's homeowners who put their hard-earned savings and creditworthiness on the line when they buy a home. It is the homeowner who maintains and improves the home. It is the homeowners who take all of the risk of owning a highly expensive asset. And yet, the residential real estate agent does none of the above and takes the 5 to 6 percent fee on size of the entire *transaction, not 5 to 6 percent of the profits.* This 5 to 6 percent fee often equates to 25 percent or more of the homeowners' profits. And yet, the broker took none of the risk, did not bear the burden of maintaining the home, or mitigate the time and mindshare stolen from the homeowner in managing the home.

Regrettably, the real estate industry has failed for decades to serve the interests of homeowners, just as in the 1980s the corporation's focus had shifted away from servicing the customer with lower costs and better products to maximizing the privileges of the corporate executives. As the second shareholder revolution spread throughout corporate America, real estate remained controlled not by shareholders/homeowners, but by insiders who continued to siphon off fat fees generally uncorrelated to their efforts, intelligence, or hours.

The reason real estate brokers could avoid not one but two consumer tsunamis, which naturally cleaned other industries of high prices and low service, is that there were not external competitive threats nor a free market where Adam Smith could do his work. Real estate brokers were essentially the last expensive intermediaries standing. The widespread adoption of internet technology dramatically lowered the buying and selling costs of nearly every asset in the U.S.—except for homes. The stock and bond markets are possibly the most obvious form of the movement toward direct-to-consumer platforms that shift power from the middleman/broker to the end consumer by empowering the consumer with information at low costs. As other examples, by connecting drivers and riders directly, Uber and Lyft displaced taxi dispatchers. By connecting travelers with transportation and accommodation options directly, sites like Expedia and Priceline.com have displaced travel agents. From matchmaking to car shopping to taxi dispatching to stock brokering, the internet has transformed nearly everything we do by reducing the cost of transacting and providing the consumer with more information and more control. If a job title or description had included the word "agent" or "broker," the web had taken over much of that person's work and their clutch on "proprietary" information. The result was much lower fees, better customer service, and in fact even an improved work environment for the intermediary.

Because only one intermediary has been immune to the power of the internet to replace much of what the middleman used to do at a great reduction in costs, evidence of an industry fix was overwhelming as exemplified by the following questions:

1. Why has only one industry of intermediaries not only had prices per unit *not* dropping, but even in the last year had prices increasing?

2. Why has only one middleman had increases in revenues which exceeded the inflation rate for seventy-three of the last seventy-five years?

3. Why would revenues increase faster than inflation in almost every year, when the costs of delivering those exact services have dropped precipitously over the years, as consumers do much of the work of the traditional agent on their own, such as the searching for homes online on their own, a process which used to take tens of hours per week with agents driving customers around in cars?

4. Why is residential real estate the last business left in America whose distribution channel is still the very expensive door-to-door sales force, made obsolete in every other industry?

5. Why have the service levels of the realtor not greatly improved along with the service levels of every other industry in the U.S.?

6. Lastly, why is the price of this service in the U.S., its economy known as the most efficient in the world, two to three times the price for the exact same service in nearly every other developed country?

Of course, the answers to the above as described in this book lie in the fact that the largest trade group in the U.S. has erected walls of monopoly around their industry. This cartel means that Adam Smith's invisible hand is helpless to impose its discipline. He can only work in free markets.

The more we looked at the housing industry, the more Lynley and I saw a problem that had to be fixed. Lynley and I therefore built REX with the goal of driving real estate commissions to near zero the way that Schwab, Expedia, and others had done. Such a result would also lower the price of the average home in America by $30,000 or so. Yet even a smaller drop in the cost of buying and selling these homes to the international average of 2 percent would return billions of dollars to American homeowners. In fact, if we take the general commissions that prevail in free real estate markets around the globe compared to the slightly less than 6 percent commission that exists inside the U.S., the wealth moved from middle-class

Americans to realtors is around $120 billion this year and about $1.5 trillion over the next ten years.

It is hard to think of a greater stimulus to the expansion of the U.S. economy, a stronger catalyst to the growth in jobs and wages of the U.S. economy, especially the trades such as plumbers, electricians, and carpenters, a faster way to reduce the cost of consuming a home when the price of every home drops by 5 to 6 percent, an increase in home building as the developers' margins improve greatly with the reduction or elimination of the realtor fee which drives the prices of homes down further as the supply of homes goes up, much more happiness for families when consumers have $120 billion extra cash in their pockets each year to spend or donate as they see fit, and greater incentives for new companies and inventors to create yet unbuilt valuable products when consumers have an extra $1.5 trillion of wealth over the next ten years. Unemployment would be permanently reduced as employers and employees could more easily match their needs to the skills of suddenly more mobile employees. The productivity of the workforce would thus also increase. Moreover, people would have an ability to freely move from place to place as their life goals, their families, and their health changes—allowing them to reach the highest fulfillment of their talents and existence. Moreover, none of this stimulus would require any money or programs from the government. In fact, tax revenues would increase untethered to any increase in government expenses, thereby lessening our deficits. The entire wealth of the nation is improved.

REX grew vertically in its early years, which means we focused on building the tools of our business rather than growing broadly across geographies. We deployed technology to automate large parts of the home-buying and -selling process, much of which is repetitive in nature so done better by robots.

As just one example, our schedule-bot removed the laborious task of coordinating the buyer, seller, and agents to schedule a time to see a home—a tedious and brain-deadening task that took up a good part of the traditional agent's job—through automated-text round robins. Innovations like this drove costs down while freeing up our salaried agents to spend time truly *serving* our clients as opposed to *selling* them. Customers became very happy. Employees, freed from monotonous tasks, enjoyed their jobs more and could devote freed up time to interacting with our customers or solving problems.

All the while, Lynley and I remained aware of the challenges that lay ahead. We knew that the major problem was that the real estate cartel would not give up the hundreds of billions of dollars of excess profits they were accumulating at the expense of middle-class Americans without a war. To accentuate the problem, the National Association of Realtors' mission statement at their founding and up until today included the goal of protecting and growing the profitability of its members. One would be hard-pressed to find another trade group that states this goal as one of the core missions, or that sets the terms of competition among its members. Those excess profits were the trade group's reason for being.

From the beginning, we refused to saddle our sellers with excessive fees. Traditional brokers sell a home by compelling the charging of *two* commissions—one that the seller pays to the seller's broker and a second commission that the seller must pay to the *buyer's* broker by order of the National Association of Realtors and their model MLS code. The arrangement is no different than if the American Bar Association were to make plaintiffs, those bringing lawsuits, also agree to pay the fees of the lawyers for the defendants on the other side of the case. Worse, by order of the National Association of Realtors, the fees of the buyer agent in real estate must be set in advance of the seller actually meeting a potential buyer, independent of whether the buyer needs an agent or not, and independent of which services the buyer would be willing to pay for if they did need an agent.

Therefore, at the time of the signing of the contract *with the seller*, the seller's agent always advises to bake in the highest possible fee for the buyer's agent, in the rare case that the best buyer is unsophisticated and needs all of the service of the most expensive buyer's agent, lest the seller lose that one buyer. As we've discussed in this book, it's a ridiculous arrangement that drives up the cost of selling a home and lines the pockets of broker firms, which are happy to collect high commissions representing buyers on deals where the sellers have been forced at the signing of the seller agreement into paying out a mandatory commission to the buyer broker. It is the Full Employment and High Wage Act for realtors.

In addition, there is the creation of a huge conflict of interest for the agent of the buyer when that buyer agent is paid by the seller. How aggressive can the defendant's lawyer be in pressing the case of the defendant when the defendant's lawyer is paid by the plaintiff after the trial ends? Same with the home buyer's agent. The buyer agent knows he is more likely to get paid a commission if he can convince the buyer to be the highest bidder for the house. This is totally opposite the ideal of putting their client first.

Moreover, as two class action lawsuits have recently alleged, the tying of these two fees into one contract is also illegal under U.S. antitrust laws. Their argument is that industry competitors agree, coordinated by the National Association of Realtors, that if you buy one service from a brokerage firm, that is the selling of a home, you must also pay for a second set of services that may not be needed, which is paying for the buyer to retain a buyer's agent whether the buyer needs one or not. Imagine going to a car dealership and being told if you buy a car from them, you must also buy a car for someone else you do not know, whether that other person even needs a car or not. By the way, the standard fee for a buyer agent is not much different than the price of a used car at the low end of the realtor fee, or a Rolls-Royce at the high end of the realtor fee so the analogy is apt.

REX did away with mandatory, fixed commissions for buyers' agents. We matched buyers and sellers directly and attached a separate licensed and salaried agent to represent the buyer at no additional cost to the seller. These salaried agents, untethered to a commission, returned tens of thousands of dollars to the home seller and the home buyer—a major step in the direction of the long-forgotten customer/shareholders in real estate—the homeowner. And if the buyer wanted to hire their own agent for some services, that decision—and what the buyer is willing to pay for those services—is up to the buyer.

Suddenly, the buyer had options. Most importantly, the buyer had negotiating leverage in choosing to work with a buyside agent on the purchase of a home if they decided to do so. These two tools were never offered to buyers before. The buyers could suddenly pay what the buyer agent was worth to them, if anything. Of course, the buyside fee dropped drastically.

Additionally, because all our agents were salaried employees, we therefore could hold our colleagues to very high service levels as one would find at Nordstrom, or Crate and Barrel, as opposed to the gig worker at our competitor firms, who could not be told what to do by law as 1099 workers. Thus, at REX, because we could create the standards of our colleagues' service levels, we continually improved our standards and our services as we learned more. We could drive customer satisfaction way up while at the same time driving our prices way down. Possibly most importantly, because our customer is the homeowner, and not the agent who is working to get the home sold as fast as possible without regard to price, or to buy the home as fast as possible for their buyer without regard to price, we got better outcomes for our home sellers or home buyers whether they were selling or buying.[102] Our agents cared about the home buyer or seller the most, and REX came second.

In what seems like magic, simultaneously the homeowner could sell their home for more while the home buyer could buy that exact same home for less. Both sides of the transaction were better off. The huge, embedded commission in the middle was removed.

Of course, no incumbent group making over $100 billion per year in excess revenues using an outdated process designed from its creation to line the pockets of the brokers wants that system to end. The hostility manifested itself in hundreds of examples of angry brokers who intimidated REX colleagues. They threatened us and our customers by often stating in shockingly direct terms that they would never take their clients to see the homes we were selling—shocking because of its breaking of their fiduciary, legal duty to their clients, in addition to the plain immorality of it. Hundreds have called us to tell us in colorful language that we are acting unprofessionally by not "cooperating," just as stock traders would do when another stockbroker would charge less than the twelve cents per share all the stockbrokers had agreed to in the 1980s and 1990s.[103] In many ways, realtors are so used to this corrupt industry practice because it has been going on for so long that they do not view their behavior as the brazen disregard of their duty to their customer, and the breaking of the law, that it is. It is a classic example of the agent, very similar to some of the CEOs of the 1980s or 1990s public companies, not focusing enough on the shareholder, or in our case, the homeowner or the home buyer, but putting themselves first because that is the only world they have known.

All along, my largest concern, however, was *not* that entrenched brokers would resist our efforts to maximize our sellers' return on their home investment. That of course was going to happen just as stockbrokers, taxi dispatchers, and travel agents resisted tech competition. More than anything, I feared the joining of forces between traditional real estate brokers and the two largest real estate technology platforms, Zillow and Trulia, which had merged after REX's launch.

I was very concerned about Zillow/Trulia turning its back on competition and being co-opted by the National Association of Realtors, even though Zillow was founded under the idea of "putting the customer first." This feeling was driven in part by the way that home aggregators such as Zillow, Trulia, Homes. com and others had trained consumers to search for houses. When Lynley and I launched REX, home shopping had been disintermediated by many websites displaying homes. Through these sites, consumers could find their next home before they ever spoke with a real estate agent. By the end of 2020, 97 percent of home shoppers used the internet to find a home. In fact, using the web was usually the first step they took. Hours and hours of the traditional brokers' work of driving people around to see homes had been removed. Yet, despite this amazing labor savings, prices stayed rigidly the same.

Because Zillow and Trulia came to represent the dominant portal through which homes were found after the FTC had allowed Zillow and Trulia to merge in 2015, I feared that real estate brokerage insiders would ultimately pressure Zillow. Zillow had made commitments to remain "independent of any real estate industry group" and to "put the customer first."

In 2022 Zillow/Trulia had about 70 percent of all apps downloaded for real estate search. Zillow had a near monopoly position and would therefore be put under tremendous pressure by the National Association of Realtors to join the cartel. In fact, both Zillow and NAR had a huge incentive to keep fees high: Zillow was dependent on advertising dollars from wealthy agents for their revenue and NAR because its goal was the (1) collection of their expensive dues from (2) as many people as possible to grow the power and compensation structures of NAR, where top executives are paid over $1 million per year.

It was clear from the real estate industry's own public comments that the industry did not want tech disruption to cut into the big broker's thick commissions. In 2015, the same year we started selling our first homes through REX, the National Association of Realtors commissioned the "DANGER report," a detailed catalogue of the trends that broker insiders feared could negatively impact the profits of the real estate industry which NAR was designed to protect.

The DANGER report is remarkable in its candor. Other industries might blush about openly discussing their power and the overt desire to do what is best for themselves over and against the needs of their customer. Big real estate brokers, by contrast, have no such inhibitions, having operated in this way in plain view for decades. This history has allowed them to become arrogant where others would be fearful, emboldened by years of invincibility. Among the "dangers" discussed by the report are a series of developments that consumers would applaud, including "Commissions Spiral Downward," "The Agent-Centric Era Ends," "Brokers Lose Control of Data," and "New Business Models Go Mainstream." But one other section caught my eye. A portion of the report discussed the industry's fear that "Technology Becomes a Runaway Train" as if technology deployed throughout its industry was a harm to be avoided. Most industries had boarded the technology train. The incumbent real estate brokers feared it.

Although Zillow was not called out by name in the section on technology platforms, the report made clear that the industry was looking closely at how to neutralize the threat of pro-consumer technology reducing broker profits. A couple years after the report was public, NAR's CEO Bob Goldberg gave an illuminating speech that further raised my concern that big real estate would try to strike a deal with the dominant tech platforms. Goldberg acknowledged that tech platforms represented a challenge. The way "to move the industry forward in our best interest," the NAR CEO explained, referring to the interest of real estate brokers, not of course homeowners, was to "identify potential alliances with external sources seeking to infiltrate" the real estate market. By "embracing" the competition, Goldberg noted, NAR could bring disruptors under the organization's tent where they would no longer pose an existential threat. He later blatantly wrote about his fear that the industry would go the way of Uber, Schwab, and Expedia, where expensive and inefficient brokerage service providers had their prices reduced by technology-driven change.

I feared that Zillow/Trulia would buckle. The platform had opened up competition because consumers could go there to find all homes whether sold by innovative brokers like REX, or the traditional incumbents. No home buyer had ever said that "they only wanted to look at homes represented by an MLS agent." Yet, aligning itself with the incumbents could bring Zillow considerable revenue because Zillow's revenue was dependent on advertising dollars from agents. If the agents' revenues and profits decreased for every customer, as would happen as brokers' commissions were reduced, the agents' willingness to pay for advertising on the Zillow platform would fall by a similar proportion. Just as I had written of the public corporations in the '80s and '90s, the real estate industry, having avoided the first two revolutions, was still aligned with the goals that the corporations came first, followed by the shareholder, and last, the customer. The revolution REX provided was to flip these priorities on their heads: take great care of the home seller or buyer first, then take great care of our colleagues at REX to make sure their jobs were rewarding, and in this way the profits and the happiness of the shareholders would necessarily follow.

My concerns reached a new level in late 2020 when Zillow announced that it was becoming a member of the National Association of Realtors and that the company would join MLS broker associations across the country. Not only was Zillow now locking arms with the industry, but we also learned that Zillow was working on redesigning its website as part of its new relationship with the traditional brokers. There was no doubt in my mind that the new website would put innovative companies lowering prices at a disadvantage. Therefore, we hurried into court to seek a preliminary injunction. With Zillow and Trulia on the brink of joining the cartel, consumers were at risk of not being able to locate all homes, just homes that were approved by the MLSs. Of course the distinction of whether a home was represented by a member of a trade group was irrelevant to the customer. Customers wanted to buy or sell a house. They did not care if the home was sold with a traditional NAR/MLS broker or not. "I only want to see a home represented by a traditional agent," said no homebuyer ever.

The collusion of the digital platforms in real estate with the industry trade group in NAR and the MLSs sought to relieve the pressure for lower prices and better services that was brought to bear on all other industries through the prior shareholder revolution in the last two decades of the last century and then the technology revolution in the first two decades of this one.

When the Zillow redesign emerged in January 2021, the cooperation with the industry trade group was even worse than I imagined in my worst nightmares. The new display moved homes not represented by members of the cartel to the virtual equivalent of Siberia—a side tab that consumers probably would not see and if they did so, only under the misleading label of "Other." All the cartel homes were under a category labeled "Agents." This label was factually wrong and damaging. Our REX colleagues were state-licensed agents, state-licensed brokers, and clearly qualified to be with all other homes based on the label of "Agents." Instead, homes sold through the industry's traditional high-commission model now received special treatment. Like segregation in the 1900s, we were not allowed to sit at the same counter.

MLS/NAR-represented homes were the default option. Those homes appeared on the screen when home shoppers plugged in a neighborhood, city, or zip code to search. Homes not sold by a cartel member were pushed to a tab that most consumers would not click, would not appear on Zillow's map that displayed homes for sale in a certain neighborhood, and worse, as mentioned, were given the suspicious title of "Other." The very collusion among vendors and incumbents that the

CEO of the NAR had literally proposed as the solution to fight off competition in the "DANGER" report had been brought to his fruition.

The effect of the Zillow web display was substantial, immediate, and harmful. Interest in our homes nosedived as views dropped by 80 percent and visits to our homes dropped by 60 percent. Our growth went from 100 percent per year on average in our first five years of existence to under 10 percent in 2022, making REX practically un-fundable. Investors do not finance smaller slow growth companies when they can buy older and safer companies growing at a similar rate. We had a much more difficult time attracting new sellers, although given the froth in the home-buying market in 2021, what homes we did list sold quickly and for high prices. Moreover, other disruptors suffered the same fate. The Zillow redesign did not just harm REX—it rendered inoperative an entire marketplace where new business models were bound to win. There used to be many homes on Zillow that were sold independent of big broker rules. All of the homes independent of the cartel, including those homes for sale by their owners, were exiled to the digital version of Siberia. Rather than competition in the industry arising, and Adam Smith being invited into the industry, the cartel had further consolidated its power and pricing, and built its fortress walls even higher.

Home sellers now knew, because the traditional agents told them, that their home would not be found online unless they got it onto the default tab of Zillow, which would only happen if their home was sold by a cartel member. As a result, the alternatives to sell one's homes outside the rules of the cartel had almost completely dried up. The realtor industry, by forcing Zillow and Trulia to play along, had blocked the handiwork of Mr. Smith to the very detriment of the people the members of the cartel were supposed to serve: home buyers and sellers. Their goal, stated in their NAR mission statement, was to maximize the profit of the agent, not the homeowners. Once again, the industry trade group had worked to obtain its objectives, keeping competition, and Adam Smith, out.

REX tried everything to overcome the coopting of Zillow and Trulia by the National Association of Realtors. We increased marketing costs to advertise around the Zillow/NAR combination. We teamed up with brokers who were members of the industry and "co-listed" properties using their credentials, so that the homes we represented would move onto the default tab of Zillow. And we ourselves joined some MLSs. None of these approaches produced the 100 percent growth, or even the 60 percent growth we achieved in the pandemic year of 2020 before the display change. They were expensive (marketing), inefficient (co-listing), and generated brand confusion (joining MLSs).

With the company operating at a greatly reduced growth rate, prior excited investors of the company grew concerned. REX, like other great disruptors, such as Uber, Lyft, Schwab, and Netflix, had grown at a 100 percent rate in our first five years. Even during COVID we grew at a 60 percent rate. But if the growth rate was 5 percent, well Proctor and Gamble, the makers of shampoos and soaps, does that at a much lower risk. Ultimately, we had to make a very difficult decision. We temporarily exited the residential brokerage business.

NAR was able to protect its fees, its service levels, and the number of NAR members, which collectively make the NAR not only the largest trade group in the U.S., but also one of the wealthiest trade groups in the country. It was an incredibly painful process. The company was forced to let go four hundred dedicated colleagues who had worked so hard and passionately to bring an honest approach to every home transaction. Our consumer satisfaction scores had been off the charts relative to our competitors and our net promoter score, another gauge of customer happiness, exceeded that of some of the most admired companies in the U.S., such as Apple, Netflix, and Microsoft. Moreover, we were achieving these atmospheric customer satisfaction scores at prices that were nearly half the price of our competitors. It was not our colleagues' fault at REX— the blame lay squarely with an industry cartel that fears putting power in the hands of the home buyers and home sellers.

Even possibly more important was that the National Association of Realtors spiked big skulls on sticks around the entire perimeter of the industry for innovators to see who may want to change it. The warning to other would-be disruptors was to not enter this industry lest they suffer the same fate as REX by daring to upset the pricing of the cartel.

Fortunately, our fight for consumers goes on. America's free market system provides entrepreneurs with wide parameters. Gratefully, our social contract is based on a legal system that prevents industry members from ganging up to advance their own profits by collectively crushing others. Business "competitors" are not allowed to work with each other to stop innovative and lower cost companies, which do business differently as the laws passed around the turn of the nineteenth century made clear under the headings of the Sherman Act and the Clayton Act. In fact, our legal system is designed to *promote* competition within industries. This competition inevitably drives innovation, higher service levels, and lower costs. To defend this competition and the values that our customers and employees stood for, we are pursuing our antitrust claims against Zillow and NAR in court. Our case is led by the famed U.S. litigator David Boies, his firm, and super-lawyer Darren McCarty.

There's an old adage that the customer is always right. In real estate, the consumer has had to deal with being told they were always wrong for decades. As I write now, I know that justice will prevail in our case. All the courts need to do is to knock down the cartel's barriers to competition and let Adam Smith and free markets do the rest. By the time this book is out, REX—and all home shoppers—will have had their day in court.

When we prevail, Adam Smith will finally be allowed into the American home. Our country will be forever changed once his invisible hand is allowed to do its work.

Freedom brought to housing will make it nearly costless to move about the country, allowing people to more easily pursue their passion, their wealth, or both. Housing markets would become much more liquid and thus less risky, increasing mobility. If more economically inclined, each worker could reach higher compensation as they moved their talents to their "highest and best use." Each entrepreneur could more easily move to the best soil for their idea. Parents could more easily move to the best place for their children and their families across the many factors they deem important. As an example, parents could move their public-schooled child to the school of their choice, helping the child, and the economy again, as the schooling of the child is more narrowly focused on the child's abilities and goals.

If there are those who view home ownership not as consumption, which we argue here, but as wealth creation through one home or the ownership of many, more people could afford the down payment and thus the purchase of assets that they believe have a great chance at price appreciation. Wealth dispersion would increase through the forced savings of the mortgage payment and the appreciation of the home.

If home ownership is instead consumption, the average home in the U.S. would come with a $20,000- to $30,000-off coupon. Even for purposes of renting, leasing rates would come down as the landlords' cost of purchasing the home asset came down. More buyers would have a real choice of renting or buying, giving them more negotiating power, as more people could afford the 15 percent to 20 percent down payment—a quarter or more of which had been needed to pay to the realtor.

Additionally, more homes would be built as the return on capital for a developer goes up, as one of the largest expense items for the builder is removed, the realtor fee, which often devours up to 20 percent of the builder's profit. Thus, the consumer of a home would get still another discount coupon to the price of the home because the greater supply of homes drives the prices of homes down again.

Laborers in all sorts of trades, such as plumbers, carpenters, electricians, and painters to name just a few, will get much more work and at much higher wages because their jobs cluster around the purchase and sale of homes. All of these trades are put to work when people first move into an existing home and tailor it to their needs or when developers hire them to build new ones. Transaction taxes will increase, which fund our first responders and educators. The number of transactions always increases dramatically as the cost of transacting drops significantly. As housing markets become more liquid, the greater number of transactions produce large increases in state transfer taxes, municipal transfer taxes, and federal capital gains taxes. They also produce more jobs, which come with payroll taxes, and higher incomes, which come with income taxes.

Our leisure time will grow as even the management of the home is outsourced to those who can manage it better and for less. New products we cannot even imagine today will be invented which, like iPhones, will improve lives in ways we cannot currently imagine. There will be excess wealth in consumer pockets, and leisure in their day, to purchase new products to the amount of $1.5 trillion over the next ten years which provides both the market and the demand for these currently un-invented new products and services. The underlying growth rate of the U.S. economy will permanently increase.

In the end, everyone can more easily reach the full flower of their potential and passions by being able to move freely about the country. These are only a few of the enormous benefits that will accrue to the wealth of the nation as the barriers to competition come down in the largest industry in the U.S.

The results are almost too fabulous to describe. That is why I am sure that the consumer will ultimately win as judges free the market from the cartel. Adam Smith will finally be welcomed into the home.

# ENDNOTES

1   Nicole Friedman and Nick Timiraos, "Housing Market Stumps Forecasters," *Wall Street Journal*, December 8, 2022

2   Nicole Friedman, "U.S. Home Sales Fall For 10th Straight Month in Row," *Wall Street Journal*, December 22, 2022

3   Heather Long, "'Soft landing' is a terrible name for what's coming," *Washington Post*, December 5, 2022

4   Anna Bahney, "All-cash offers are king in this hysterical real estate market," CNN.com, June 2, 2021

5   Niall Ferguson, *The Ascent of Money*, The Penguin Press, 2008, p. 230

6   Ibid., p. 247

7   Board of Governors of the Federal Reserve System (Community Reinvestment Act)

8   Editorial, "Sorry, Hillary, You and Bill – Not Tax Cuts – Caused the Financial Crisis," *Investor's Business Daily*, September 28, 2016

9   Vikas Bajaj and David Leonhardt, "Tax Break May Have Helped Cause Housing Bubble," *New York Times*, December 18, 2008

10  Ibid.

11  Sebastian Mallaby, *The Man Who Knew: The Life and Times of Alan Greenspan*, Penguin Press, 2016, p. 205

12  Ibid., p. 205

13  Morton Kondracke and Fred Barnes, *Jack Kemp: The Bleeding-Heart Conservative Who Changed America*, Sentinel, 2015, p. 224

14  Ibid., p. 233

15  Ferguson, *The Ascent of Money*, p. 267

16  Mallaby, *The Man Who Knew*, p. 604

17  Marc Drogin, *Anathema! Medieval scribes and the history of book curses*, A. Schram, 1983, p. 31

18  Ibid., p. 73

19  Adam Smith, *The Wealth of Nations*, Scribner's Modern Library, p. 371

20  Matt Grossman and Alison Sider, "United Plans to Buy 15 Supersonic Planes," *Wall Street Journal*, June 3, 2021

21  R. Glenn Hubbard and Christopher J. Mayer, "Low-Rate Mortgages Are the Answer," *Wall Street Journal*, December 17, 2008

22  Paul La Monica, "The undeniable bright spot in the pandemic economy," CNN Business, September 14, 2020

23  Smith, *The Wealth of Nations*, p. 320

24  Scott Smith, "Jeff Bezos Boldly Fails So Amazon Can Thrive," *Investor's Business Daily*, November 29, 2019

25  Ibid.

26  Mallaby, *The Man Who Knew*, p. 208

27  Ibid., p. 208

28  Ibid., p. 218

29  Ibid., p. 238

30  George Gilder, *Wealth and Poverty*, Basic Books, 1981, p. 176–77

31  Ibid., p. 176–77

32  Smith, *The Wealth of Nations*, p. 15

33  Ibid., p. 370

34  Ibid., p. 101

35  Ferguson, *The Ascent of Money*, p. 261

36  Andy Kessler, "Trump Could Be the First Silicon Valley President," *Wall Street Journal*, February 3, 2017

37  Stephen A. Schwarzman, *What It Takes: Lessons In Pursuit of Excellence*, Avid Reader Press, 2019, p. 249

38  Smith, *The Wealth of Nations*, p. 466

39  David Frum, *How We Got Here*, Basic Books, 2000, p. 291

40  Ibid., p. 292

41  Mike Martin, Chloe Baker, and Charlie Hatch-Barnwell, *Crossing the Congo*, Hurst, 2013, p. 129

42  Ibid., p. 28

43  Ibid., p. 23, 28

44 Ibid., p. 2

45 Ibid., p. 27

46 Ibid., p. 4

47 Ibid., p. 153

48 John D. Gartner, *The Hypomanic Edge*, Simon & Schuster, 2005

49 Lawrence Wright, *God Save Texas*, Knopf, 2018, p. 202

50 Smith, *The Wealth of Nations*, p. 3

51 Ibid., p. 5

52 Reuven Brenner, "How the Financial Crisis Did Not Change the World," *Foreign Affairs*, Spring 2019, Volume III, No. 1

53 Richard C. Morais, "Even the Chefs Are Leaving France," *Forbes*, November 30, 1998

54 Greg Steinmetz and Matt Marshall, "How a Chemicals Giant Goes About Becoming a Lot Less German," *Wall Street Journal*, February 18, 1997

55 Enrico Moretti, *The New Geography of Jobs*, 2012, Houghton Mifflin Harcourt, p. 49

56 Ibid., p. 60

57 Jack Ryan, "Why Are House Sales Such a Bad Deal for Every American?" *RealClearMarkets*, November 27, 2020

58 Roger Alford and Benjamin Harris, "Anticompetition In Buying and Selling Homes," *Regulation Magazine*, Summer 2021

59 Kevin Baker, *America the Ingenious*, Artisan, 2016, p. 140

60 Susan Strasser, "What's In Your Microwave Oven?", *New York Times*, April 14, 2017

61 Steven Hayward, *The Age of Reagan: The Fall of the Old Liberal Order, 1964-1980*, Forum Prima, 2001, p. 290

62 Baker, *America the Ingenious*, Artisan, p. 71–72

63 Michael Toth, "Warning to the Real-Estate Cartel," *Wall Street Journal*, July 8, 2021

64 Alford and Harris, "Anticompetition In Buying and Selling Homes"

65 Ibid.

66 Moretti, *The New Geography of Jobs*, p. 154–55

67 Jackie Caradonio, "Travel Agents Are Back: Here Are 4 Expert Companies Ready to Craft Your Dream Trip," *Robb Report*, July 23, 2019

68 T.A. Heppenheimer, *Turbulent Skies*, Wiley, 1995, p. 8

69  Warren Brookes, *The Economy In Mind*, Universe Books, 1982, p. 152–53

70  Caradonio, "Travel Agents Are Back"

71  Amber Gibson, "The Father-Daughter Duo Behind the World's Most Expensive Vacations," *Forbes*, April 17, 2019

72  Katherine Clarke, "These YouTubers Are Lifting the Veil On America's Most Expensive Homes," *Wall Street Journal*, April 29, 2021

73  Elisabetta Povoledo, "It's Fast, Hot and Cheesy, But Will Romans Bite?" *New York Times*, June 8, 2021

74  Steven Russolillo, "Amazon's IPO at 20: That Amazing Return You Didn't Earn," *Wall Street Journal*, May 14, 2017

75  Nick Wingfield and Patricia Cohen, "Amazon Plans Second Headquarters, Opening a Bidding War Among Cities," *New York Times*, September 7, 2017

76  Taylor Soper and Monica Nickelsburg, "Amazon tops 75,000 employees in Seattle area," *GeekWire*, January 6, 2021

77  Moretti, *The New Geography of Jobs*, p. 75–76

78  Doug Kass, "Some Really Stupid Things Uttered By Some Really Smart People," *RealClearMarkets*, June 29, 2017

79  Ibid., p. 60

80  Peter Thiel and Blake Masters, *Zero to One*, Currency, 2014, p. 188

81  Ibid., p. 66

82  Ali Wolf, "The Housing Boom Doesn't Help Everyone," *New York Times*, July 13, 2021

83  David Harrison, "Low-Wage Workers Hit Harder by Layoffs," *Wall Street Journal*, May 15, 2020

84  Wolf, "The Housing Boom Doesn't Help Everyone"

85  Parul Sehgal, "The Water Even Corroded GM's Engines," *New York Times*, July 4, 2018

86  Joe Gose, "Investors Fear Losing a Prized Loophole," *New York Times*, June 9, 2021

87  Ibid.

88  S.L. Price, *Playing Through the Whistle*, Atlantic Monthly Press, 2016, p. 314

89  Jared Diamond, "How Ohtani Is Besting the Babe," *Wall Street Journal*, July 13, 2021

90 Ibid.

91 Gray Rohrer and Beth Kassab, "DeSantis task force to restart Florida economy looks to overcome coronavirus 'psychology of fear,'" *Orlando Sentinel*, April 20, 2020

92 Edward Pinto, "Coronavirus, and the Media's Lies, Damned Lies, and Statistics," *RealClearMarkets*, April 14, 2020

93 Rohrer and Kassab, "DeSantis task force to restart Florida economy"

94 Amelia Josephson, "The Economics of Disney World," *SmartAsset*, May 21, 2018

95 Patricia Mazzei and Manny Fernandez, "'All In, All the Time': Reopening Florida Schools Is Likened to a Military Operation," *New York Times*, August 19, 2020

96 Sareen Habeshian and Mary Beth McDade, "Mayor Garcetti announces water and power will be shut off for nonessential L.A. businesses that don't close," KTLA5, March 24, 2020

97 Madeline Wells, "Newsom's office says to keep masks on between bites when eating out," SFGate, October 3, 2020

98 Paul Watkins, "U.S. States Must Team Up If They Want To Compete w/ California," *RealClearMarkets*, May 21, 2021

99 Ibid.

100 Chris DeVore, "Silicon Valley Keeps Winning Because Non-Competes Limit Innovation," TechCrunch, February 8, 2016

101 Timothy B. Lee, "A little-known California law is Silicon Valley's secret weapon," Vox, February 13, 2017

102 Steven D. Levitt and Stephen J. Dubner, *Freakonomics: A Rogue Economist Explores the Hidden Side of Everythihng,* William Morrow, 2005, p. 20–36

103 *United States v. Alex Brown & Sons, Inc.*, 169 F.R.D. 532 (S.D.N.Y. 1996)

# ACKNOWLEDGMENTS

## BY JOHN TAMNY

<hr>

I'll start with Jack Ryan, and his indefatigable lieutenant in an attempt to bring reason to the housing space, Michael Toth. Michael was persistent in bringing Jack and me together on one of those "Zoom calls" back in 2020, only for Jack to express his desire to bring Adam Smith into the home. I'd long wanted to write a book about housing, and Smith was the perfect muse.

Big thanks go to my wife Kendall. Through her own relentless searching for housing, she revealed to me in bright colors just how dated the traditional commission structure for realtors is. Kendall is an ongoing inspiration to whom I'm very grateful, as am I grateful to Claire and Reed, our seven-and-a-half-year-old and four-year-old children. We're very lucky.

Bob Reingold is mentioned in all of my books, and with good reason. Notable on the housing front is that he had great success in creating his own housing and building supply businesses, plus he's done very well in real estate itself. The argument made within the book about unspent wealth as the driver of nearly all progress has Bob's fingerprints all over it.

Jeff Yass has so many weighty things to do, and people to discuss important issues with, but he always makes time for me.

Ed Crane, the co-founder of the Cato Institute, has made time for me going back to 2003 when I went to work for him. He literally and figuratively raises an eyebrow to much of what I write and say, but I remind him that much of what I write and say is informed by his own thinking.

Howie Rich converses with me in Crane-like fashion. With good reason, I suppose. My views are strident, and frequently odd. Despite this, Howie still takes my calls. Howie is the personification of doer, and a role model to me for being a doer.

Hall McAdams has been patiently mentoring me for twenty years. When my confidence was low, Hall took me and my contrarian thoughts seriously. I hate to think where I'd be today if Hall hadn't taken a meeting with me in October of 2003.

Hall heads the board of my new venture, the Parkview Institute. Bob Landry is the other board member with Hall. Bob is so smart, but also so supportive. Writing in the way I do, I've earned myself a lot of critics. Bob routinely comes to my defense, and lifts me when I need it. I'm very lucky to work with Hall and Bob.

Ken Fisher's writing on the stock market and the economy help explain my boundless optimism. I've got so much to say, but around Ken I frequently go quiet simply because he fascinates me. I've learned so much from Ken, but most of all I've learned to relax. Ken isn't alarmed by things. He routinely finds the proverbial silver lining in calm fashion, all the while acknowledging the "Dark Ages" that capitalists routinely out-run. Like Crane, Ken has taught me how to think.

Richard Masson still returns my e-mails after all these years about people, sports, currencies, wines, business, and the brilliant individuals he's worked with in finance. He could so easily be aloof, but always takes the time to explain things to me. As much as I've asked him, I have so much more to ask. And ask I will.

Vickie-Love Greenlee provided crucial information to me about the evolution of the travel industry, from agents to counselors. Vickie-Love and her mother Victoria Greenlee have lived the transformation of the travel industry, and their experiences helped shape the arguments made in favor of unfreezing realtor commissions. Mark Nojaim's commentary on travel was similarly very useful. Nojaim plans remarkable global excursions for his clients much like Vickie-Love, and they're both real-world examples of the brilliant progress that results when professions leave the past behind.

Steve Forbes remains the person I want to be but fall short of being. It's not just that I've learned so much from him about economic policy; it's from how he interacts with people that I've learned the most. I want to carry myself as he does, and so does Kendall want me to carry myself as he does.

Kim Dennis, Richard Tren, and Courtney Myers of the Searle Foundation continue to support my work, and even better, they continue to make me think I'm funny and interesting. Spending time with them is a joy, as is it joyful telling them how lucky I am to do the work I do. They've long helped to make my work possible, and I hope they know how grateful I am.

Big thanks go to Anthony Ziccardi and Maddie Sturgeon of Post Hill Press. Anthony expressed enthusiastic interest in *Bringing Adam Smith into the American Home* when we brought the manuscript to him, and then Maddie has been wonderfully energetic ever since. She's a great person with whom to bring a manuscript to print.

Last, but surely not least, I'd like to thank my parents, Peter and Nancy, along with my sister Kim. I'm incredibly lucky to have them. They've literally watched me grow up, and have been very supportive despite watching me grow up.